SPECTRUM®
Science
Test Practice

Grade 3

Published by Spectrum®
an imprint of Carson-Dellosa Publishing
Greensboro, NC

Spectrum®
An imprint of Carson-Dellosa Publishing LLC
P.O. Box 35665
Greensboro, NC 27425 USA

Printed in the OH USA • All rights reserved.   ISBN 978-0-7696-8063-7

02-152127784

SCIENCE TEST PRACTICE
Table of Contents
Grade 3

Science Test Practice is for everyone who wants to have a working knowledge of the fundamentals of science. Written with the goal of helping students achieve on science tests, it approaches science through the format of the National Science Education Standards.

The National Science Education Standards were developed by the National Academy of Science, an organization of the leading scientists in the United States. Their goal is for all students to achieve scientific literacy. To be scientifically literate means to be able to understand the richness of the world around us; to be able to make decisions based on the skills and processes that science teaches us; and to approach problems and challenges creatively.

This book is divided into sections, each one based on a National Science Education Content Standard. Through the Pretest, you will see where the student's strengths and challenges lie. Then the student will be exposed to each content area through the course of the book. Finally, a Posttest will show you and the student how much he or she has improved.

Each section begins with a brief description of the Content Standard covered within. This book focuses on the content standards A-D: science inquiry, physical science, life science, and Earth/space science. The remaining content standards, which cover science and technology and science in personal and social perspectives, are covered within the other four sections. A correlation chart details the coverage of all standards in the book (see pp. 8-9).

Students can begin with the Pretest (pp. 10–14). This test covers all three major strands of science:

- physical science, which includes how objects move and interact;

- life science, which includes animals, plants, and ecosystems;

- earth and space science, which includes rocks and minerals, the oceans, and the solar system.

After the Pretest, you may wish to complete the test practice pages in order, or complete the sections out of sequence. The pages generally deal with specific topics within the field—for example, ecosystems or the rock cycle.

Finally, the Posttest gives the student a chance to practice yet again, applying the knowledge gleaned from the rest of the book. A complete answer key appears at the back.

With its real-life questions and standards-based approach, *Science Test Practice* will engage students; give them solid test-taking hints and practice; and provide them an opportunity to build their confidence for other exams.

Dear Parent or Guardian,

Taking a test can be one of the most stressful things your child does. With today's increased emphasis on tests in school, that stress is greater now than ever. How can you help your child?

Practice will help a lot. This book will give your child plenty of practice with multiple-choice, short-answer, and extended-response questions. Every multiple-choice question gives four possible choices. One is the best answer. Short-answer questions require a very brief response. Extended-response questions ask your child to respond in full sentences and usually to provide a more complete answer than short-answer questions.

Try working out the questions with your child. As you and your child complete the multiple-choice questions, explore what makes the incorrect answers wrong. The short-answer questions require a brief response; usually these can be answered in a sentence or two. The extended-response questions can be answered in different ways each time. They draw upon your child's understanding of a concept and challenge his or her writing skills. After your child responds, share your ideas about the question. It will help your child learn that there is more than one way to approach a problem.

But science is about more than tests. You might find something that sparks your child's interest. Try out an experiment together, or read about different kinds of animals. Take a walk outside under the moon, or use a mirror to reflect light in different paths. Science is about asking questions and searching for answers. You don't need to be a scientist to help your child be successful at mastering this content.

Remember: you are your child's first and most important teacher.

National Science Education Content Standards Correlation

Each national content standard begins with the phrase, "As a result of activities in grades K–4, all students should develop . . ."

Standard	Pages
CONTENT STANDARD A: Science as inquiry	
Abilities necessary to do scientific inquiry	10, 13, 16–22, 31, 40, 73, 90
To learn about the world in a scientific manner, students need to learn how to ask questions, formulate possible answers, devise experiments to test those answers, and base their conclusions on evidence.	
Understanding about scientific inquiry	10, 13, 16–23, 25, 31, 40, 73, 90
Students need to understand that the investigations used to gather information depend on the question being asked; that scientists use mathematics and technology as they work; and that scientists build on the work other scientists have done, by asking questions about that work and that grow out of that work.	
CONTENT STANDARD B: Physical Science	
Properties of objects and materials	10–12, 18–19, 21–23, 28–33, 72, 85, 87, 89–90
Position and motion of objects	14, 18, 33–34, 37, 66, 82–84, 90
Light, heat, electricity, and magnetism	22, 33–35, 65, 76, 83, 85–86, 90
CONTENT STANDARD C: Life Science	
The characteristics of organisms	10, 12–13, 39–49, 53–54, 56–60, 87, 89
Life cycles of organisms	11, 13, 40–50, 52
Organisms and environments	10–13, 25-26, 40, 42–49, 51, 53, 55–61, 71, 73, 87
CONTENT STANDARD D: The Earth and Space Science	
Properties of Earth materials	10, 12, 31, 36, 55, 65–73, 81, 87, 89
Objects in the sky	11, 14, 18, 35, 49, 65, 74–80, 82–86, 89–90
Changes in the earth and sky	11, 12, 14, 53, 65, 67–72, 74-83, 85, 87-88, 90

National Science Education Content Standards Correlation

CONTENT STANDARD E: Science and Technology	
Abilities of technological design	12–13, 21, 23, 31, 33–36, 61, 63, 74–75, 86, 88, 90
Understanding about science and technology	11–12, 14, 16, 18, 21, 24, 33–36, 61, 63, 75, 80, 88
Ability to distinguish between natural objects and objects made by humans	11–13, 36, 75, 80-81, 89
CONTENT STANDARD F: Science in Personal and Social Perspectives	
Science can seem removed from everyday life, but it actually surrounds us. Personal hygiene activities are based in scientific reasoning. Understanding the risks and benefits in the world makes students more informed citizens.	
Personal health	35, 51, 62, 76, 81, 86
Populations, resources, and environments	12, 25–26, 39, 43–44, 54, 59, 71–72
Natural hazards	11–12, 33, 35–36, 56, 63, 65, 80–81, 87, 89
Risks and benefits	11–12, 36, 54–55, 58, 60, 68, 71, 75, 80–81, 90
Science and technology in society	11–13, 17, 35, 54, 75, 81
CONTENT STANDARD G: History and Nature of Science	
Science as a human endeavor	78–79
Science is a pursuit of human beings, with many different skills, backgrounds, qualities, and talents. However, scientists all share curiosity about the world, a tendency to ask questions about what is known, an openness to new ideas, insight, and creativity.	

Name_____ Date_____

Directions: Read the questions. Choose the truest possible answer. Shade in the circle before your choice.

Example:
a. Which of the following is a mammal?
- Ⓐ gorilla
- Ⓑ butterfly
- Ⓒ chicken
- Ⓓ jellyfish

---

1. **Bobby wants to measure the mass of a rock. Which unit should he use?**
   - Ⓐ gram → mass
   - Ⓑ liter → liquid → water, milk, juice
   - Ⓒ pound → mass
   - Ⓓ meter → length.

2. **Kelly measures the volume of a piece of wood. What does she want to know?**

   L x W x h.
   - Ⓕ how big it is
   - Ⓖ how much it weighs
   - Ⓗ how old it is
   - Ⓙ how rough it is

3. **What four things do all animals need to survive?**
   - Ⓐ food, water, shelter, air
   - Ⓑ sunlight, food, water, feathers
   - Ⓒ fur, sunlight, shelter, food
   - Ⓓ shelter, soil, water, fur

4. **What are atoms?**
   - Ⓕ grains of sand
   - Ⓖ large plants
   - Ⓗ tiny pieces of matter
   - Ⓙ small animals

5. **The Giant Panda is an herbivore. What foods does the Giant Panda eat?**

   - Ⓐ animals only
   - Ⓑ plants only
   - Ⓒ animals and plants
   - Ⓓ rotting animals and plants

GO ON

mixture vs Solution.

Name_____ Date_____

Directions: Read the questions. Choose the truest possible answer. Shade in the circle before your choice.

6. **Jin is making iced tea. He adds sugar to the tea. The sugar dissolves into the tea and disappears. What has Jin made?**

   Ⓕ a mixture
   Ⓖ an atom
   Ⓗ an element
   Ⓙ a solution

7. **Where does coal come from originally?**

   Ⓐ It is made by scientists in a laboratory.
   Ⓑ It erupts from volcanoes.
   Ⓒ It forms on the forest floor when trees die.
   Ⓓ It forms underground from the remains of plants.

8. **After a rainy day, Carlos notices puddles in his backyard. After two warm, sunny days, Carlos sees that the puddles have disappeared. It rains again and the rain makes new puddles. What is Carlos seeing?**

   Ⓕ life cycle
   Ⓖ water cycle
   Ⓗ food web
   Ⓙ condensation

9. **What is this diagram called?**

   Sunflowers   Mouse   Owl

   Ⓐ food pyramid
   Ⓑ food web
   Ⓒ energy pyramid
   Ⓓ food chain

10. **What is caused by the earth's rotation on its axis?**

   Ⓕ mountains
   Ⓖ earthquakes
   Ⓗ thunder
   Ⓙ day and night

11. **Tyrone's family takes cans, bottles, and plastic bags to a recycling center every Saturday. What is recycling?**

   Ⓐ making something new from old, used materials
   Ⓑ throwing away containers in a place that will not hurt the environment
   Ⓒ burning some kinds of trash so it does not fill up landfills
   Ⓓ burying trash in the the earth so it is out of the way

Grade 3 Pretest

Directions: Read the questions. Choose the best word to fill in the blank. Shade in the circle before your choice.

Example:
b. The smallest part of matter is a(n) _____ .

- Ⓐ bit
- Ⓒ atom
- Ⓑ digit
- Ⓓ egg

12. **Animals are sorted into groups by their _____ .**
    - Ⓐ ages
    - Ⓑ ability to fly
    - Ⓒ blood types
    - Ⓓ physical features

13. **All of the living and nonliving things that interact in an environment form a(n) _____ .**
    - Ⓕ habitat
    - Ⓖ community
    - Ⓗ ecosystem
    - Ⓙ population

14. **A car burns gasoline to _____ .**
    - Ⓐ power the engine
    - Ⓑ change radio stations
    - Ⓒ use the windshield wipers
    - Ⓓ turn the steering wheel

15. **A(n) _____ is when the earth's surface shakes.**
    - Ⓕ volcano
    - Ⓖ earthquake
    - Ⓗ flood
    - Ⓙ hurricane

Directions: Read the question. Write a short answer on the space provided.

16. **Name three properties of matter that you can see.**
    Color, Shape, length.

17. **What are three ways that you can conserve resources?**
    Turn off water, Drive less, use less ligth

GO ON

Name_____ Date_____

Directions: Read each question. Write a paragraph that answers each one on the lines provided. Use a topic sentence. Be sure to end every sentence with a period.

18. **You win a dream field trip to the ecosystem of your choice. Tell which ecosystem you would choose and why. What do you expect to see, do, and learn on your trip?**

_____

_____

_____

| **Possible ecosystems:** |
| rainforest, tundra, ocean, temperate forest, desert, river, lake, pond |

_____

_____

_____

_____

19. **You notice that, each night, a streetlamp turns off at a different time. Develop a question, hypothesis, and experiment about the lamp.**

_____

_____

_____

_____

_____

_____

_____

GO ON

Directions: Read the text below and study the diagram. Use information from both to help you answer questions 20–22.

Just as the earth revolves around the sun, the moon revolves around the earth. It takes about one month for the moon to make a complete revolution, or trip, around the earth. From the earth, the moon seems to change shape over the course of the month. This is because different parts of the moon are lit up by the sun as the moon passes by the earth.

Before calendars were invented, people used the shapes of the moon to tell what day and month it was. We can still do that today. The shapes of the moon are always in the same order and follow a cycle over the course of a month. So even if you do not have a calendar, if you know the cycle of the moon, you can tell what time of the month it is.

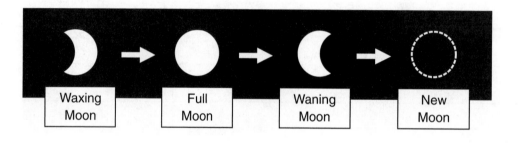

20. **What are the different shapes of the moon called?**
    - (A) sessions
    - (B) rotations
    - (C) revolutions
    - (D) phases

21. **During a waning moon, _____ .**
    - (F) part of the moon is invisible
    - (G) part of the moon falls off
    - (H) the whole moon is visible
    - (J) the whole moon is hidden

22. **You know that, in a given year, on January 20, there is a full moon. You also know that on February 21, there is another full moon. When can you expect another full moon?**
    - (A) February 28
    - (B) March 1
    - (C) March 10
    - (D) March 21

Content Standard A

The first section of the National Science Education Standards concerns science and its contemporary application. First, students will learn what science is and which principles, processes, and concepts science incorporates. Second, students will use their critical thinking skills and use science in a way that is not only informative, but also allows them to apply what they learn to solve problems.

Perhaps most importantly, students will learn to ask questions about the world from a scientific perspective. Asking questions is the very root of science.

━━━━━ Grade 3 ━━━━━

Directions: Read the text below. Use the information to help you answer questions 1–2.

HINT: Read the questions first. Then read the passage and underline parts that might answer the questions.

Raheem decided to set up an experiment. "I'll grow three plants. I'll put one plant near music, one near talking people, and one in silence. I bet the plant next to music will grow fastest."

Raheem planted three of the same kind of plant. He put one plant next to the radio in the kitchen. He put one next to the TV in the living room. He put the last one in his bedroom. He made sure the plants all got the same amount of light and water. Raheem made sure that the TV and radio were both on at the same volume for exactly one hour each day. He was very quiet near the plant in the bedroom. Every day, Raheem measured each plant and recorded how much it had grown.

After two weeks, Raheem made a chart. It showed how much each plant had grown each day. The plant near the radio grew the fastest. The plant in the quiet bedroom grew the most slowly.

"My study shows that music is better for plants than talking," he wrote. "But talking is better than silence."

1. Which was Raheem's hypothesis?

- Ⓐ "I'll grow three plants."
- Ⓑ "I'll put one near music, one near talking people, and one in silence."
- Ⓒ "I bet the one next to music will grow fastest."
- Ⓓ "My study shows that music is better for plants than talking."

2. How did Raheem record his data?

- Ⓕ He asked his family not to watch television near the plants.
- Ⓖ He made a video of each of the plants growing.
- Ⓗ He measured the plants each week.
- Ⓙ He wrote down how much each plant grew each day.

Directions: Use the Word Bank to fill in the sequence map.

1.

┌─────────────────────── **Word Bank** ───────────────────────┐
│   theory   hypothesis   experiment   question   │
└──┘

☐ → ☐ → ☐ → ☐

Directions: Read the question. Write your answer on the line provided.

2. **Why is it important to form a question before performing an experiment?**

_____

_____

3. **Karen said, "I have a theory. I think that hair grows faster in summer than in winter." Explain to Karen why her idea is a hypothesis and not really a theory.**

_____

_____

_____

Directions: Read the questions. Choose the truest possible answer. Shade in the circle before your choice.

4. **What should Karen do to test her hypothesis?**
   - (A) set up an experiment
   - (B) cut her hair only in winter
   - (C) ask her friends what they think
   - (D) tell her teacher her hypothesis

5. **What is a possible experiment that Karen can run to test her hypothesis?**
   - (F) check to see if her hair is longer in summer or winter
   - (G) get her hair cut more often
   - (H) measure how fast her hair grows
   - (J) measure her hair and a friend's hair and compare results

🛑 STOP

Name_____ Date_____

Directions: Read the questions. Choose the truest possible answer. Shade in the circle before your choice.

HINT: Answer the questions you know first. Then go back and answer the questions that are more difficult.

1. **Jenna lets go of a party balloon. She watches it rise into the sky and disappear. What is a scientific question she might have?**

   Ⓐ How much did that balloon cost?

   Ⓑ What color was that balloon?

   Ⓒ How high did my balloon go?

   Ⓓ Would my sister like a balloon, too?

2. **What kinds of questions are good for testing?**

   Ⓕ boring questions

   Ⓖ those that already have answers

   Ⓗ those you are interested in

   Ⓙ unimportant questions

3. **Mr. James shows his class that he can stand an egg on its end. He says, "Today is the only day of the year I can do this." What is a good scientific question his class might ask?**

   Ⓐ Where did you get that egg?

   Ⓑ Why is today the only day you can do that?

   Ⓒ Can I eat that egg when you are done?

   Ⓓ Where did you learn that neat trick?

4. **Teddy wants to see how much his bean plant grows during the week. Which tool should he use to take measurements?**

   Ⓕ a clock

   Ⓖ a measuring cup

   Ⓗ a ruler

   Ⓙ a thermometer

GO ON

Directions: Read the text below and study the chart. Use information from both to help you answer questions 1–6.

The metric scale is a way to measure objects. It describes weights and measures based on the meter (m), liter (L), and gram (g). You can change the measures into larger or smaller ones by using a prefix. If you add hecto- to meter, you have a hectometer, which equals 100 meters.

Kilo-	1,000
Hecto-	100
Deca-	10
Centi-	1/100
Milli-	1/1,000

1. **Ashley's dad entered a 100-km bicycle race. What does the abbreviation "km" stand for?**
   - (A) liter
   - (B) kilometer
   - (C) centimeter
   - (D) kilogram

2. **Lauren saw that a can of soda had 45 mg of the substance caffeine in it. What does the abbreviation "mg" stand for?**
   - (F) milligram
   - (G) millimeter
   - (H) metergram
   - (J) megagram

3. **Brett measured a 10-cm block of wood. What does the abbreviation "cm" stand for?**
   - (A) mile
   - (B) kilometer
   - (C) centimeter
   - (D) cubic meter

4. **How many meters are there in a decameter?**
   - (F) 10
   - (G) 50
   - (H) 100
   - (J) 1,000

5. **How many liters are in a kiloliter?**
   - (A) 5
   - (B) 10
   - (C) 100
   - (D) 1,000

6. **A gram is about the mass of a paper clip. Which of these objects is about a decagram in weight?**
   - (F) a pencil
   - (G) a turkey
   - (H) a person
   - (J) a car

STOP

Name_____ Date_____

Directions: Read the text below and study the diagram. Use information from both to help you answer the questions.

A ruler is a tool that helps measure the size of an object. Rulers usually have marks for the units of inches and centimeters. Measuring accurately is an important part of science.

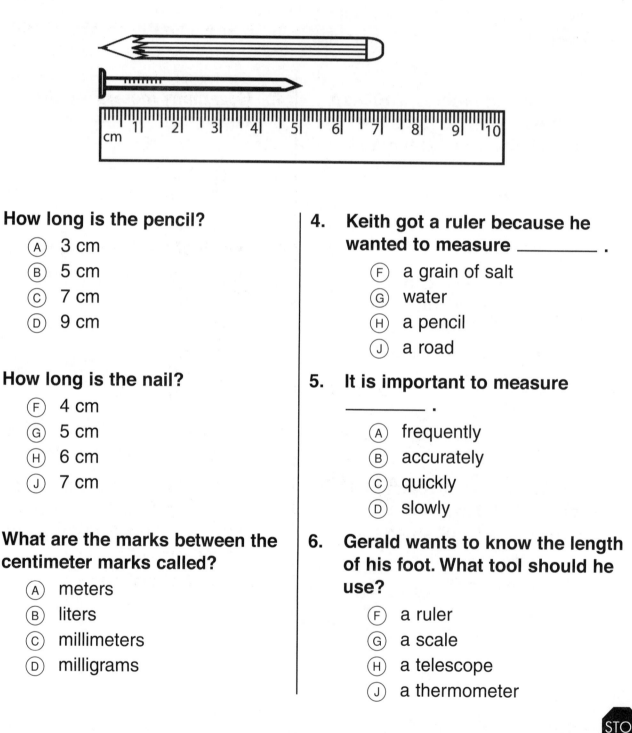

1. **How long is the pencil?**
    - (A) 3 cm
    - (B) 5 cm
    - (C) 7 cm
    - (D) 9 cm

2. **How long is the nail?**
    - (F) 4 cm
    - (G) 5 cm
    - (H) 6 cm
    - (J) 7 cm

3. **What are the marks between the centimeter marks called?**
    - (A) meters
    - (B) liters
    - (C) millimeters
    - (D) milligrams

4. **Keith got a ruler because he wanted to measure _____ .**
    - (F) a grain of salt
    - (G) water
    - (H) a pencil
    - (J) a road

5. **It is important to measure _____ .**
    - (A) frequently
    - (B) accurately
    - (C) quickly
    - (D) slowly

6. **Gerald wants to know the length of his foot. What tool should he use?**
    - (F) a ruler
    - (G) a scale
    - (H) a telescope
    - (J) a thermometer

STOP

Name_____ Date_____

Directions: Study the diagram. Use information from it to help you answer the questions.

HINT: If you have trouble reading a problem, put each sentence into your own words. It can help you figure out what is difficult about the question.

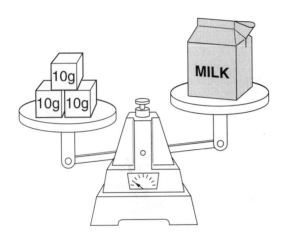

1. **Which is heavier—the blocks or the milk carton?**

_____

2. **Patty took one milk carton and put it in the left pan of the balance. Then she put another milk carton on its side in the right pan of the balance. Which way will the arrow point?**
   - (A) to the left
   - (B) to the right
   - (C) straight up
   - (D) straight down

3. **If you take the carton of milk off the balance, what will happen to the mass of the carton of milk? Why?**

_____

_____

_____

4. **Which of the following is too light to be measured on a balance?**
   - (F) an atom
   - (G) a pencil
   - (H) a deck of cards
   - (J) a hamster

5. **Which of these should you place directly on the pan of the balance?**
   - (A) hot objects
   - (B) powder chemicals
   - (C) liquid chemicals
   - (D) a cool container

Name_____ Date_____

Directions: Read the questions. Choose the truest possible answer. Shade in the circle before your choice.

1. **What does a thermometer measure?**
   - Ⓐ time
   - Ⓑ temperature
   - Ⓒ weight
   - Ⓓ volume

2. **What two systems of measurement do we use to measure temperature?**
   - Ⓕ alpha and beta
   - Ⓖ inches and meters
   - Ⓗ gallons and liters
   - Ⓙ Celsius and Fahrenheit

Directions: Read the question. Write your answer on the line provided.

3. **Give three reasons it is important to know the temperature.**

   _____

   _____

   _____

Directions: Study the diagram below. Use the information to help you answer question 4.

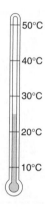

4. **What is the temperature on the thermometer above?**
   - Ⓐ 0 degrees Celsius
   - Ⓑ 15 degrees Celsius
   - Ⓒ 25 degrees Celsius
   - Ⓓ 50 degrees Celsius

5. **The lower the temperature, the _____ it is.**
   - Ⓕ hotter
   - Ⓖ colder
   - Ⓗ more humid
   - Ⓙ less humid

Grade 3

Directions: Read the text below and study the diagram. Use information from both to help you answer questions 1–2.

Volume measures how much space something takes up. It is a physical property of solids, liquids, and gases. You can measure a liquid, like water, with a measuring cup. You can measure a solid, like a brick, with a ruler. It is difficult to measure a gas, like air, because the volume can easily change.

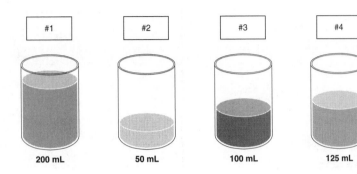

1. **Which jar has the largest volume of liquid?**

   (A) #1
   (B) #2
   (C) #3
   (D) #4

2. **Which jar has the smallest volume of liquid?**

   (F) #1
   (G) #2
   (H) #3
   (J) #4

3. **Ruby needs to find a new aquarium for her pet fish. Carlos has an old aquarium, but it is a different shape. How can Ruby and Carlos figure out if Carlos's aquarium is larger than Ruby's old one?**

   _____

   _____

   _____

4. **Why can't you use a ruler to measure the volume of water?**

   _____

   _____

   _____

Name_____ Date_____

Grade 3

Directions: Read the questions. Choose the truest possible answer. Shade in the circle before your choice.

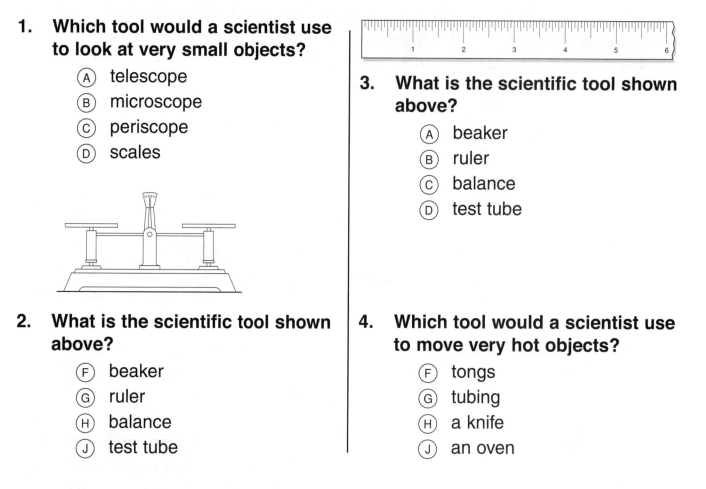

1. **Which tool would a scientist use to look at very small objects?**
   - (A) telescope
   - (B) microscope
   - (C) periscope
   - (D) scales

3. **What is the scientific tool shown above?**
   - (A) beaker
   - (B) ruler
   - (C) balance
   - (D) test tube

2. **What is the scientific tool shown above?**
   - (F) beaker
   - (G) ruler
   - (H) balance
   - (J) test tube

4. **Which tool would a scientist use to move very hot objects?**
   - (F) tongs
   - (G) tubing
   - (H) a knife
   - (J) an oven

Directions: Read the questions. Write your answer on the lines provided.

5. **Name two small tools scientists use.**

_____

_____

6. **Name two large tools scientists use.**

_____

_____

STOP

Name_____ Date_____

Directions: Study the chart. For questions 1–5, draw bars on the chart to show the information.

Diving Duck Population In North America

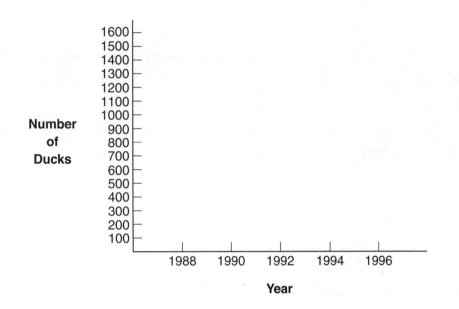

1. **In 1988, there were 800 diving ducks in North America.**

2. **In 1990, there were 500 diving ducks.**

3. **In 1992, there were 800 diving ducks.**

4. **In 1994, there were 700 diving ducks.**

5. **In 1996, there were 1400 diving ducks.**

Directions: Use information from the chart to help you answer question 6.

6. **Who might be most interested in reading this chart?**

   Ⓐ someone studying what ducks eat

   Ⓑ someone interested in getting a duck for a pet

   Ⓒ someone who wants to know where ducks live

   Ⓓ someone studying how animal populations change

Name_____ Date_____

Directions: Read the text below and study the diagram. Use information from both to help you answer the questions. Shade in the circle before your choice.

Erin was working on a science project. She went to the lake each day. She counted all the ducks that visited. Soon, she had all the information she needed to finish her project.

Erin got to work making a bar graph to show the results. She put the names of the duck groups on the bottom line of her graph. Then she put numbers on the line that went up the side. The numbers showed the number of ducks. She drew the bars that showed how many ducks she saw from each group. Last, she gave her graph the title, "Duck Population of Our Local Lake."

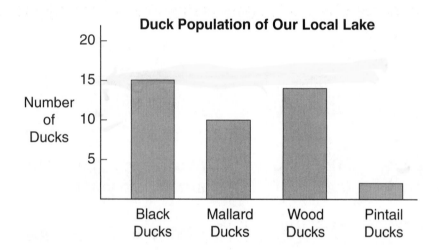

1. **Which kind of duck visited the lake most often?**
   - (A) black
   - (B) mallard
   - (C) wood
   - (D) pintail

2. **How many pintail ducks did Erin see during her research?**
   - (F) 1
   - (G) 5
   - (H) 9
   - (J) 14

3. **What were the groups of data that Erin compared?**
   - (A) kinds of ducks
   - (B) duck feathers
   - (C) different lakes
   - (D) different days

Content Standard B

Section B of the National Science Education Standards presents information about the properties of objects and materials, the motion of objects, light, heat, electricity, and magnetism. This section concerns physical science.

Some of this section focuses on material objects and how they exist in the physical world from their density, mass, volume, and state to their reaction to liquids and energy. Going further, this section explores the science behind magnetism, electricity, force, and motion.

Students will observe physical objects firsthand as they begin to understand the way the physical world works.

Name_____ Date_____

Directions: Read the text below. Use the information to help you answer the questions. Shade in the circle before your choice.

HINT: Put an X on any answers you know are wrong. Then choose the best answer from the ones that are left.

If you took a piece of aluminum foil and cut it in half, both parts would still be aluminum. If you cut one side in half again, it would still be aluminum. In fact, if you kept cutting, it would still be aluminum all the way down to the aluminum atom. An atom is the smallest piece of matter. All matter is made of atoms. Grass, oceans, this book, and even you are made up of atoms. They are much too small to be seen.

1. **The whole piece of aluminum foil is made of _____ .**
   - (A) an aluminum atom
   - (B) many aluminum atoms
   - (C) a water atom
   - (D) many water atoms

2. **In which state of matter are atoms usually closest together?**
   - (F) solid
   - (G) liquid
   - (H) gas
   - (J) steam

3. **Where would you find atoms?**
   - (A) only in solids
   - (B) only in liquids
   - (C) only in gases
   - (D) in solids, liquids, and gases

4. **If you add energy to atoms, _____ .**
   - (F) they get closer
   - (G) they move more quickly
   - (H) they stop moving
   - (J) they die

5. **Matter is anything that takes up space and has _____ .**
   - (A) heat
   - (B) color
   - (C) shape
   - (D) mass

Name_____ Date_____

Grade 3

Directions: Read the text below and study the chart. Use information from both to help you answer questions 1–4. Shade in the circle before your choice.

HINT: Sometimes it's easier to see a problem. Use blank space next to a question to make a drawing.

A physical property is a quality you can measure about a substance. Color is a physical property. So is size. You can change a substance's physical properties without changing what the substance is. For example, you can roll a sheet of paper into a ball. Although its shape is different, it is still paper. You can use physical properties to identify objects, too.

Physical Properties of Substances

	Color	Shape	Size
Peas	green	round	small
Thyme Leaves	green	flat	small
Popcorn	yellow	round	small
Grapes	green	round	large

1. **Kim needs to identify the small, round, green objects she has. According to the table, what are they?**
   - Ⓐ peas
   - Ⓑ thyme leaves
   - Ⓒ popcorn
   - Ⓓ grapes

2. **Gary has small, green, flat objects. What are they?**
   - Ⓕ peas
   - Ⓖ thyme leaves
   - Ⓗ popcorn
   - Ⓙ grapes

3. **Which physical property differs between peas and grapes?**
   - Ⓐ color
   - Ⓑ shape
   - Ⓒ size
   - Ⓓ none of the above

4. **How does popcorn differ from peas?**
   - Ⓕ color
   - Ⓖ size
   - Ⓗ shape
   - Ⓙ none of the above

Name_____ Date_____

Directions: Look at each picture. Tell which physical property of matter is being changed. Shade in the circle before your choice.

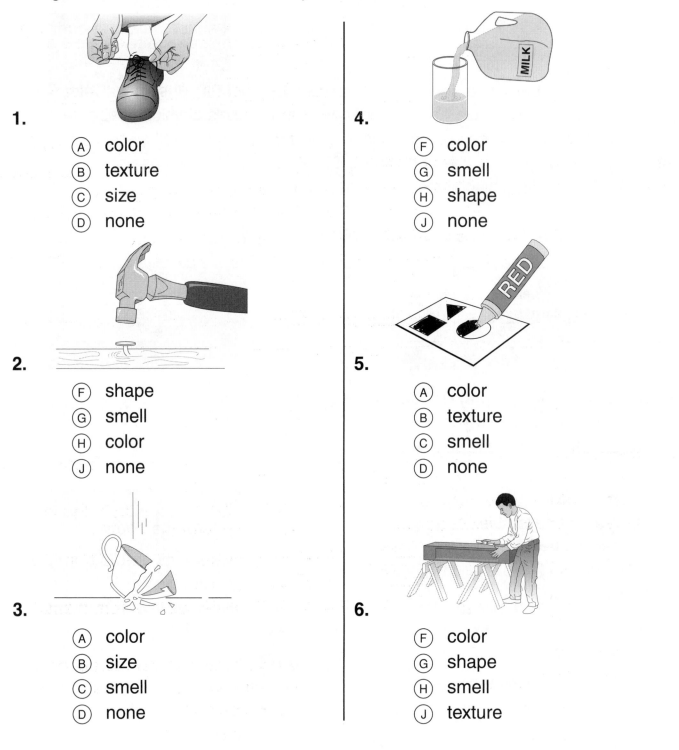

1.
- Ⓐ color
- Ⓑ texture
- Ⓒ size
- Ⓓ none

2.
- Ⓕ shape
- Ⓖ smell
- Ⓗ color
- Ⓙ none

3.
- Ⓐ color
- Ⓑ size
- Ⓒ smell
- Ⓓ none

4.
- Ⓕ color
- Ⓖ smell
- Ⓗ shape
- Ⓙ none

5.
- Ⓐ color
- Ⓑ texture
- Ⓒ smell
- Ⓓ none

6.
- Ⓕ color
- Ⓖ shape
- Ⓗ smell
- Ⓙ texture

Directions: Read the questions. Choose the truest possible answer. Shade in the circle before your choice.

1. **Milk is a _____ .**
   - (A) gas
   - (B) solid
   - (C) liquid
   - (D) steam

2. **A piece of wood is a _____ .**
   - (F) gas
   - (G) solid
   - (H) liquid
   - (J) steam

3. **The air we breathe is a _____.**
   - (A) gas
   - (B) solid
   - (C) liquid
   - (D) steam

4. **Kendra has a substance. She takes it from one container and puts it into another with a different shape. The shape changes, but the volume stays the same. What does she have?**
   - (F) liquid
   - (G) solid
   - (H) gas
   - (J) steam

Directions: Read the text below and study the diagram. Use information from both to help you answer questions 5–6.

Umi fills two glass jars with 30 milliliters of water each. She puts a lid on one but not the other. The next day, Umi measures the volume of water in each jar. This is what she finds:

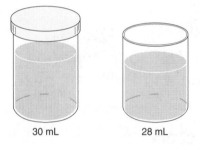

30 mL   28 mL

5. **Why is there less water in one jar?**
   - (A) Water evaporated from the jar with no lid.
   - (B) Water melted from the jar with no lid.
   - (C) Water evaporated from the jar with a lid.
   - (D) Water melted from the jar with a lid.

6. **If Umi puts a lid on the second jar, what will the volume of water be tomorrow?**
   - (F) 0 mL
   - (G) 28 mL
   - (H) 30 mL
   - (J) 32 mL

STOP

Name_____ Date_____

Directions: Read the text below and study the diagram. Use information from both to help you answer the questions.

Penelope stirs a spoon of sugar into a clear glass of water. The sugar is dissolved, or completely mixed, in the water. She has just made a solution. The dissolved sugar is the solute. The water is called a solvent.

Philip stirs a spoonful of sand into his glass of water. The sand does not dissolve. When Philip stirs the sand in the glass, the water swirls the sand around. When he does not stir the sand, it settles on the bottom of the glass. Philip has just made a mixture.

1. **Why is Penelope's glass a solution and Philip's a mixture?**

    (A) because Philip's glass is clear and Penelope's is not

    (B) because Philip's water was colder than Penelope's

    (C) because the sand did not dissolve into the water

    (D) because the sand is heavier than the sugar

2. **What else could Philip have put into his glass and made a mixture?**

    (F) lemon juice

    (G) sand and chalk

    (H) water and ice cubes

    (J) sugar cubes and white sugar

3. **Which of the following is another example of a mixture?**

    (A) salad

    (B) gold

    (C) water

    (D) salt

4. **If chocolate is dissolved in milk, milk is the _____ .**

    (F) solvent

    (G) mixture

    (H) solute

    (J) gas

5. **If chocolate is dissolved in milk, chocolate is the _____ .**

    (A) solvent

    (B) mixture

    (C) solute

    (D) gas

STOP

Grade 3

Directions: Use the words in the Word Bank to complete the passage.

Word Bank
stored   the sun   heat   fossil fuels

Energy is all around us. The food we eat, the batteries we use, and the fossil fuels

we burn are all kinds of **1.** _____ energy. Energy from **2.** _____ is

held in the food we eat. **3.** _____ hold energy from tiny animals and plants

that lived millions of years ago. Stored energy is released as **4.** _____ .

Directions: Read the questions. Choose the truest possible answer. Shade in the circle before your choice.

5. **What is energy?**
   - (A) the ability to do work
   - (B) the outer layer of the earth
   - (C) an object's weight
   - (D) how well a boat can float

6. **Jack turns on a lamp in his bedroom. How does the energy get to it?**
   - (F) sunlight
   - (G) air waves
   - (H) wind power
   - (J) electrical current

Directions: Read the text below and study the diagram. Use information from both to help you answer question 7.

7. **Rashad made a flashlight using a cardboard tube, aluminum foil, a light bulb, and a batteries. Which part is the source of energy?**
   - (A) cardboard tube
   - (B) aluminum foil
   - (C) light bulb
   - (D) batteries

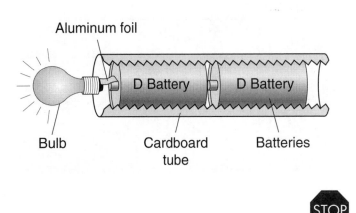

Aluminum foil

D Battery   D Battery

Bulb   Cardboard   Batteries
                 tube

STOP

Grade 3

Directions: Read the questions. Choose the truest possible answer. Shade in the circle before your choice.

1. **What happens as you move farther from a light source?**
   - Ⓐ The light gets brighter.
   - Ⓑ The light bends.
   - Ⓒ The light gets dimmer.
   - Ⓓ The light becomes clearer.

2. **Tavon's mom said, "The man driving behind us has his lights on very bright!" She was driving the car and facing forward. How did she see the lights behind her?**
   - Ⓕ She saw the lights in the mirrors in her car.
   - Ⓖ She saw the lights shining on the sides of her car.
   - Ⓗ She saw the lights in the front window of her car.
   - Ⓙ She saw the lights on the car in front of her.

Directions: Use information from the diagram to help you answer question 3.

3. **Why does a light bulb shine light in more directions than a flashlight?**

   _____

   _____

   _____

   _____

   _____

   _____

   _____

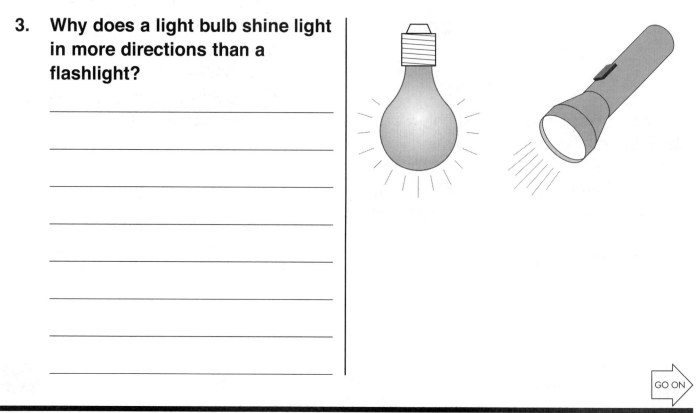

GO ON

Directions: Read the questions. Choose the truest possible answer. Shade in the circle before your choice.

4. **Paul's house uses solar panels to make electricity. How do solar panels make electricity?**

    (A) They burn natural gas in a big tank.

    (B) They collect and store energy from sunlight.

    (C) They connect all electrical equipment together.

    (D) They reflect energy from sunlight and wind.

5. **Electricity can flow easily through _____ .**

    (F) insulators

    (G) conductors

    (H) rubber

    (J) plastic

6. **Ellen is an electrician. She needs to connect electrical wires together in a building. What material should her gloves be made of?**

    (A) thick metal

    (B) thin cloth

    (C) thin aluminum foil

    (D) thick rubber

7. **What is a very safe thing Ellen can do before she begins working with wires?**

    (F) turn off the electrical current to the wires

    (G) make sure the wires are carrying current

    (H) wear a special hat that conducts electricity

    (J) cover the door to the house with rubber

Name_____ Date_____

Directions: Read the questions. Choose the truest possible answer. Shade in the circle before your choice.

1. **A fossil fuel is a source of energy that comes from tiny plants and animals that were once alive. What are the three major forms of fossil fuels?**
   - Ⓐ water, rocks, plastic
   - Ⓑ coal, oil, natural gas
   - Ⓒ carbon, gas, ice
   - Ⓓ dirt, charcoal, vapor

2. **How is oil found?**
   - Ⓕ by drilling into the earth
   - Ⓖ by boiling water
   - Ⓗ by mixing dirt with salt
   - Ⓙ by mixing chemicals in a lab

3. **Once fossil fuels are gone, _____ .**
   - Ⓐ we just make more
   - Ⓑ they will return in a little while
   - Ⓒ they cannot be replaced
   - Ⓓ there will be no more energy

4. **When were the fossil fuels that we use today formed?**
   - Ⓕ one hundred years ago
   - Ⓖ one thousand years ago
   - Ⓗ ten thousand years ago
   - Ⓙ millions of years ago

Directions: Read each question. Write your answers on the lines provided.

5. **Why do we call them "fossil fuels"?**

_____

_____

6. **Fossil fuels are nonrenewable. Name three sources of power that are renewable.**

_____

_____

_____

Name_____ Date_____

Grade 3

Directions: Read the question and study the picture. Use the picture to help you answer question 1. Write your answer on the lines provided.

1. **Jenica is at bat in a baseball game. Name three examples of motion that might occur while she plays.**

   _____

   _____

   _____

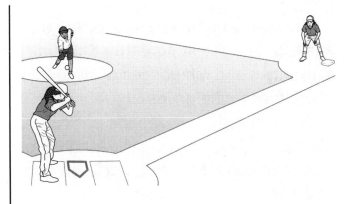

Directions: Read the questions. Choose the truest possible answer. Shade in the circle before your choice.

2. **What is required to move any object?**
   - Ⓐ thought
   - Ⓑ force
   - Ⓒ air
   - Ⓓ speed

3. **How fast something is moving is called _____ .**
   - Ⓕ motion
   - Ⓖ distance
   - Ⓗ time
   - Ⓙ speed

4. **Force is a _____ .**
   - Ⓐ distance
   - Ⓑ push or pull
   - Ⓒ motion
   - Ⓓ speed

5. **Maya and her dog are pulling on the same toy. The toy does not move because _____ .**
   - Ⓕ Maya's force is the same as her dog's force.
   - Ⓖ Maya's force is more than her dog's force.
   - Ⓗ Maya's force is less than her dog's force.
   - Ⓙ Maya has force, but her dog has none.

6. **What force acts on all objects on the earth?**
   - Ⓐ gravity
   - Ⓑ speed
   - Ⓒ distance
   - Ⓓ acceleration

Content Standard C

Section C of the National Science Education Standards focuses on plants, animals, and the living earth. Students will be introduced to the scientific similarities and differences of living things and encouraged to think critically about these differences.

Students will examine the basic needs and structures of living things in an attempt to determine what distinguishes living things from each other and how they interrelate. Students will learn about ecosystems and how organisms live and survive on the earth.

From understanding consumers and producers to examining food webs and adaptation, students will receive a basic overview of organisms and their life functions that will prove vital in the study of science.

Name_____ Date_____

Directions: Read the text below. Use it to help you answer the questions.

HINT: When a question has a passage, underline the parts that seem important. Also, underline any facts you learn.

Miss Goodman asked her students to think about what makes plants different from animals.

"I know!" said Jenny. "Plants are green."

Fatima thought for a few seconds. "But frogs and snakes are green," she said.

Jenny said, "What other differences can there be?"

Fatima said, "Animals eat plants and other animals."

Jenny added, "And plants use water and soil and sunlight to make their own food. Could that be the difference?"

"It sounds like you two came up with an excellent answer!" said Miss Goodman.

1. **What did Jenny and Fatima decide was the difference between plants and animals?**

   _____

   _____

2. **Why did Fatima think that the difference between plants and animals was not that plants are green?**

   _____

   _____

3. **What is another difference that Fatima could have suggested?**

   _____

   _____

Name_____ Date_____

Directions: Read the questions. Choose the truest possible answer. Shade in the circle before your choice.

HINT: One of the questions on this page asks you to compare and contrast two pictures. Make sure to think about both pictures when you answer.

1. **Oak trees, roses, and mosses are all similar because they are** _____ .

   Ⓐ animals
   Ⓑ cells
   Ⓒ plants
   Ⓓ herbivores

2. **Where don't plants usually live?**

   Ⓕ in the ocean
   Ⓖ on rocks
   Ⓗ on sheets of plastic
   Ⓙ in a muddy swamp

3. **What are the leaves on a pine tree called?**

   Ⓐ bark
   Ⓑ cones
   Ⓒ branches
   Ⓓ needles

4. **How are the items in the two pictures the same?**

   Ⓕ They are both bunches of leaves.
   Ⓖ They are both covers for seeds.
   Ⓗ They both fall off only in the winter.
   Ⓙ They both change colors in the fall.

Directions: Read the question. Write your answer in a complete sentence on the lines provided.

5. **Calvin filled a jar with soil and planted a seed in it. He watered the soil and then placed a lid on top of the jar. He put the jar in his front yard. The seed started to grow, but stopped. Which of the plant's basic needs did Calvin forget?**

_____

_____

GO ON

Name_____ Date_____

Directions: Study the diagram below. Use words from the Word Bank to fill in the missing labels.

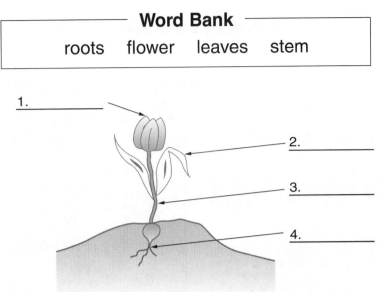

Word Bank

roots   flower   leaves   stem

1._____

2._____

3._____

4._____

Directions: Read the questions. Choose the truest possible answer. Shade in the circle before your choice.

5. The _____ of a plant carries water and nutrients from the roots to other parts of the plant.
   - Ⓕ leaf
   - Ⓖ stem
   - Ⓗ seed
   - Ⓙ flower

6. A plant's roots help to _____ .
   - Ⓐ hold the plant in the ground
   - Ⓑ send water to the rest of the plant
   - Ⓒ get nutrients from the soil
   - Ⓓ all of the above

7. The trunk of a tree is really its _____ .
   - Ⓕ leaf
   - Ⓖ root
   - Ⓗ seed
   - Ⓙ stem

8. What is the most important job that leaves do?
   - Ⓐ collect water
   - Ⓑ shade roots
   - Ⓒ make food
   - Ⓓ protect branches

Name_____ Date_____

Directions: Read the questions. Choose the truest possible answer. Shade in the circle before your choice.

HINT: If you don't know the answer, try filling in each word to see if it makes sense. Put an X on words that don't make sense in the sentence.

1. **Plants use _____, water, and carbon dioxide to make their own food.**

    Ⓐ sunlight

    Ⓑ soil

    Ⓒ flowers

    Ⓓ oxygen

2. **Plants make their own food in a process called _____ .**

    Ⓕ photosynthesis

    Ⓖ respiration

    Ⓗ germination

    Ⓙ reproduction

3. **Most of the food in a plant is made in the _____ .**

    Ⓐ flowers

    Ⓑ leaves

    Ⓒ seeds

    Ⓓ sunlight

4. **Leaves contain _____, which makes them look green.**

    Ⓕ chlorophyll

    Ⓖ seeds

    Ⓗ sugar

    Ⓙ water

5. **Give two ways that plants can spread their seeds.**

    _____

    _____

    _____

6. **Fill in the boxes with the word plant, seed, and seedling in the order that describes a plant's life cycle.**

 0-7696-8063-1—*Science Test Practice*

Grade 3

Directions: Read the questions. Choose the truest possible answer. Shade in the circle before your choice.

1. **All animals _____ .**
   - (A) lay eggs
   - (B) have four feet
   - (C) make their own food
   - (D) get food from plants or other animals

2. **An animal that eats only plants is a(n) _____ .**
   - (F) herbivore
   - (G) carnivore
   - (H) omnivore
   - (J) insectivore

3. **Which is an animal?**
   - (A) vine
   - (B) robot
   - (C) bacteria
   - (D) fish

4. **A Venus flytrap is an organism that can make its own food. It also eats insects. What kind of organism is it?**
   - (F) animal
   - (G) plant
   - (H) insect
   - (J) herbivore

Directions: Read the questions. Write your answers on the lines provided.

5. **How do animals get energy?**

   _____
   _____
   _____

6. **What does it mean when an animal is extinct?**

   _____
   _____
   _____

Directions: Study the diagram below. Use words from the Word Bank to fill in the missing labels.

1.

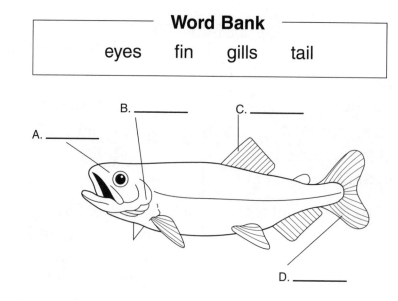

━━━━━━ **Word Bank** ━━━━━━
eyes   fin   gills   tail

A. _____

B. _____

C. _____

D. _____

Directions: Read the questions. Choose the truest possible answer. Shade in the circle before your choice.

2. **How do most fish reproduce?**

(F) They give birth to live young.

(G) They lay eggs in the water.

(H) They build nests and let eggs hatch.

(J) They release spores.

3. **Which body part allows fish to get the oxygen they need from water?**

(A) tail

(B) gills

(C) lateral line

(D) scales

Directions: Read the question. Write your answer on the lines provided.

4. **Why is it bad for fish when people pollute rivers?**

_____

_____

_____

STOP

Name_____ Date_____

Directions: Read the questions. Choose the truest possible answer. Shade in the circle before your choice.

HINT: If you don't know the answer to a question, you can sometimes get clues from the questions around it. For example, question 1 can help you answer question 2.

1. **Jamal was walking on a bridge over a stream. As he looked out over the stream, Jamal saw a creature he had never seen before. The creature was sitting on a rock in the sun. It had dry skin and scales. What kind of animal did Jamal see near the stream?**

    Ⓐ a fish
    Ⓑ a bird
    Ⓒ a reptile
    Ⓓ a mammal

2. **What is the biggest difference between amphibians and reptiles?**

    Ⓕ Reptiles have two sets of eyes and amphibians have one.
    Ⓖ Reptiles are usually green and amphibians are brown.
    Ⓗ Reptiles can live in water and amphibians cannot.
    Ⓙ Reptiles can live in dry climates and amphibians cannot.

3. **Reptiles and amphibians are**
    _____ .

    Ⓐ egg-layers
    Ⓑ very noisy
    Ⓒ very rare
    Ⓓ good swimmers

4. **How long have amphibians lived on the earth?**

    Ⓕ since 1960
    Ⓖ since 1100
    Ⓗ for several thousand years
    Ⓙ for hundreds of millions of years

5. **Which is the same of both fish and reptiles?**

    Ⓐ They both live underwater.
    Ⓑ They both have gills.
    Ⓒ They are both vertebrates.
    Ⓓ They are both found in deserts.

Directions: Read the questions. Choose the truest possible answer. Shade in the circle before your choice.

1. **What are three traits of birds?**
   - (A) All birds build nests, lay eggs, and eat meat.
   - (B) All birds fly, have teeth, and have two legs.
   - (C) All birds have feathers, two legs, and wings.
   - (D) All birds have wings, have teeth, and build nests.

2. **Why do many birds build nests?**
   - (F) to protect their eggs
   - (G) to store food
   - (H) to use up spare twigs
   - (J) to hibernate all winter

3. **Midori is studying a bird that is perched in a tree. The bird is red with black patches over its eyes. It is probably a _____ .**
   - (A) penguin
   - (B) ostrich
   - (C) cardinal
   - (D) seagull

4. **Alejandro finds two bright blue eggs on the ground near his home. What should he do?**
   - (F) pick them up and take them to his teacher
   - (G) build a nest up in a tree and put the eggs in it
   - (H) bring them to his house and put them in a towel
   - (J) leave them alone and wait to see if the mother bird returns

Directions: Read the questions. Write your answers on the lines provided.

5. **What is one trait that reptiles and birds have in common?**

_____

6. **Give three reasons feathers are important to birds.**

_____

_____

_____

STOP

Name_____   Date_____

Directions: Read the questions. Choose or write the truest possible answer.

HINT: Try each answer out. If you can think of a time when the answer is not right, don't choose that answer. For example, in question 1, can you think of a mammal that is not very large?

1. **Mammals are _____ .**
   - (A) hairy
   - (B) egg-layers
   - (C) very large
   - (D) very small

2. **Which is a specific trait of mammals?**
   - (F) They have fur or hair.
   - (G) They provide milk for their young.
   - (H) They maintain their own body temperature.
   - (J) all of the above

3. **What trait is the same for mammals, birds, and reptiles?**
   - (A) They all lay eggs.
   - (B) They all have fur.
   - (C) They all have a backbone.
   - (D) They are all warm-blooded.

4. **A whale is a mammal. What is different about a whale than most other mammals?**
   - (F) Whales do not produce milk.
   - (G) Whales do not live on land.
   - (H) Whales lay eggs.
   - (J) Whales have fur.

5. **Which of these animals is a mammal?**

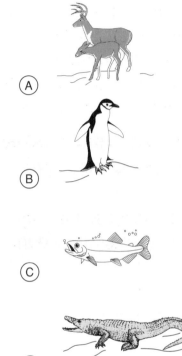

6. **Oscar finds an animal. It lives in the woods and lays eggs. It has four legs, two eyes, and scales. It has a backbone and it eats plants. Give two reasons why Oscar decides that this animal is NOT a mammal.**

_____

_____

_____

Name_____   Date_____

Directions: Read the text below. Use the information from it to help you answer the questions.

Tanesha and her family are at the beach. Her brother, Deandre, finds a shell. "What is this?" he asks.

Tanesha replies, "It's a shell. Some invertebrates have shells like this to protect themselves. They also need something to support their bodies. People have backbones and bones to hold up their bodies."

"Wow!" cries Deandre. "What animal did this come from?"

"Well," says Tanesha. "It can't be an oyster shell, because it's not very flat. It might have been a snail's shell. Let's leave it here in case a hermit crab needs a new home!"

1. **What is the main difference between vertebrates and invertebrates?**
    - (A) Vertebrates live on land.
    - (B) Invertebrates lay eggs.
    - (C) Vertebrates have a backbone.
    - (D) Invertebrates can fly.

2. **Based on the passage, what is a snail?**
    - (F) an invertebrate
    - (G) a vertebrate
    - (H) a fish
    - (J) a mammal

3. **Which kind of invertebrate has a shell?**
    - (A) ladybug
    - (B) jellyfish
    - (C) oyster
    - (D) spider

4. **A turtle has a shell and it lays eggs. However, it is a reptile and not an invertebrate. Why?**
    - (F) because it cannot fly
    - (G) because it takes care of its young
    - (H) because it has a backbone
    - (J) because it does not have feathers

5. **Give one reason why an elephant is NOT an invertebrate.**

    _____

    _____

    _____

Name_____ Date_____

Directions: Read the questions. Choose the truest possible answer. Shade in the circle before your choice.

1. **What are the basic needs of all animals?**

   Ⓐ food, plants, oxygen, and carbon dioxide

   Ⓑ fish, food, plants, and carbon dioxide

   Ⓒ the sun, water, shelter, and oxygen

   Ⓓ food, water, shelter, and oxygen

2. **Which is an example of shelter?**

   Ⓕ a rabbit burrow

   Ⓖ stripes on a zebra

   Ⓗ an owl eating a mouse

   Ⓙ a fish swimming in a lake

3. **Which two things are parts of air?**

   Ⓐ food and oxygen

   Ⓑ carbon dioxide and oxygen

   Ⓒ oxygen and claws

   Ⓓ carbon dioxide and food

4. **Why do all land animals need oxygen?**

   Ⓕ to breathe

   Ⓖ to stay warm

   Ⓗ to help them change sunlight into food

   Ⓙ to keep them safe from other animals

5. **How do birds reproduce?**

   Ⓐ Birds lay eggs and hatch chicks.

   Ⓑ Birds give birth to live chicks.

   Ⓒ Birds find nests with eggs in them.

   Ⓓ Birds don't reproduce at all.

6. **Each animal has traits, or physical features, from _____.**

   Ⓕ only their mothers

   Ⓖ only their fathers

   Ⓗ both their mothers and fathers

   Ⓙ neither their mothers nor fathers

GO ON

Name_____ Date_____

Directions: Use words in the Word Bank to fill in the passage below.

Word Bank

lay eggs   fertilized   born   reproduce

You may know that some animals, like lizards and fish, **1.** _____ .

Actually, most animal life begins with an egg. In some animals, like deer and

rabbits, an egg is present in its mother from birth. It must be

2. _____ to become an embryo, or an early form of a baby. The

embryo grows inside its mother until it is **3.** _____ . At least some of

any species must **4.** _____ , or the species will die out.

Directions: Read the text below. Use the information to help you answer the questions.

HINT: If you get stuck on a question, go on to the next one. Mark the one you skipped in your test book so you can come back to it later.

Many animals have defenses that help protect them from other animals. The stinky smell from a skunk is a kind of defense. Teeth and claws are other kinds of defense. Plants have defenses, too. If you have ever pricked your finger on a rose stem, you have felt a plant's defense.

1. **Which is a good example of a defense?**
   - Ⓐ a bear catching a fish
   - Ⓑ an owl flying home
   - Ⓒ a snake showing its fangs
   - Ⓓ a mouse stealing food

2. **Where can grass in a field get fresh water?**
   - Ⓕ from a running stream
   - Ⓖ from the ocean
   - Ⓗ from a lake
   - Ⓙ from rain

3. **People need shelter from harsh conditions. Which conditions are harsh?**
   - Ⓐ snowy, stormy weather
   - Ⓑ mild, cloudy weather
   - Ⓒ calm, sunny weather
   - Ⓓ bright, sunny weather

4. **Which is an example of a predator?**
   - Ⓕ a dog eating from its bowl
   - Ⓖ a rabbit eating a carrot
   - Ⓗ a robin eating a worm
   - Ⓙ a blackbird eating a berry

5. **Give another example of a defense.**

   _____

   _____

   _____

Name_____ Date_____

Directions: Study the diagram below. Use words in the Word Bank to fill in the missing labels.

HINT: Get a good night's sleep before any big test. Sleep and a good breakfast can help you think more clearly.

Word Bank

tadpole   egg   young frog   adult frog

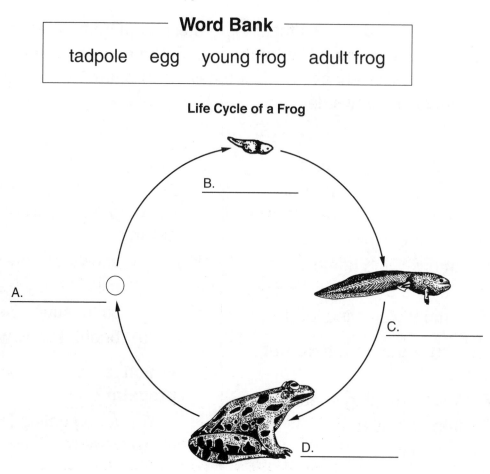

Life Cycle of a Frog

B. _____

A. _____

C. _____

D. _____

Directions: Study the diagram above. Use the information to help you answer questions 2–3.

2. **What does the frog have that the tadpole does not have?**
   - Ⓐ gills
   - Ⓑ legs
   - Ⓒ eyes
   - Ⓓ a tail

3. **What is the diagram above called?**
   - Ⓕ life cycle
   - Ⓖ rock cycle
   - Ⓗ water cycle
   - Ⓙ system cycle

STOP

Name_____ Date_____

Directions: Read the questions. Choose the truest possible answer. Shade in the circle before your choice.

HINT: Question 6 asks for a lot of information. If you do not know the whole answer to the question, write whatever you do know.

1. **Which animal are you most likely to see in a forest?**
   - Ⓐ camel
   - Ⓑ dolphin
   - Ⓒ squirrel
   - Ⓓ penguin

2. **Which kind of plant are you most likely to see in a forest? (Remember that trees with woody stems grow in forests.)**
   - Ⓕ tall grass
   - Ⓖ oak tree
   - Ⓗ cactus
   - Ⓙ tomato plant

3. **Remember that all life requires water, air, and food. Which area will probably have the least plant and animal life?**
   - Ⓐ temperate forest
   - Ⓑ desert
   - Ⓒ river
   - Ⓓ rain forest

4. **Why do very few plants grow in the desert?**
   - Ⓕ The soil is dry and there is little water.
   - Ⓖ The weather is much too hot at day and night.
   - Ⓗ There is too much rainfall.
   - Ⓙ There are not enough animals.

5. **Which animal is most likely to survive in the desert?**
   - Ⓐ frog
   - Ⓑ crab
   - Ⓒ coyote
   - Ⓓ dolphin

Directions: Read the questions. Write your answers on the lines provided.

6. **Would more animals live in a forest with lots of water or very little water? Why?**

   _____

   _____

   _____

   _____

   _____

Name_____ Date_____

Directions: Read the text below. Use the information to help you answer the questions.

People, animals, and weather can change ecosystems. When a beaver builds a dam, it changes a stream into a pond. Many animals and plants are able to use the water in a pond. But the water no longer flows. The animals and plants that used the old stream must adapt.

Natural events can change ecosystems. Floods, fires, and tides can change the soil in an area. Some plants need different soils to survive. If plants die off, many animals can die, too. People can change ecosystems as well. When we cut down trees to make paper, we change the land. Making roads, building houses, and farming are large ways that people change ecosystems.

1. **Which is an example of a natural event that changes an ecosystem?**

    Ⓐ Chemicals from a factory run into a lake.

    Ⓑ People cut all the trees down from an area.

    Ⓒ Heavy rain makes mud slide down a mountain.

    Ⓓ Farmers plow a field to make farmland.

2. **How might a snowy ecosystem change if the temperature grew warmer?**

    Ⓕ More animals would adapt to have white fur.

    Ⓖ More plants could grow in the soil.

    Ⓗ More fish would try to live on the land.

    Ⓙ More snow would fall to change the ecosystem back.

3. **Which of the following is LEAST likely to change an ecosystem?**

   (A) hunting season moved back by one day

   (B) a campfire burns out of control and becomes a fire

   (C) a new highway cuts through land

   (D) all of the insect-eating birds leave

4. **If people dumped chemicals into the water source of an ecosystem, what is the FIRST thing that would happen?**

   (F) The animals would not have enough plants and clean water.

   (G) Plants that live there would thin out or stop growing.

   (H) The chemicals would pollute the water and soil.

   (J) Some plants and animals would begin to adapt.

Directions: Read the question. Write a paragraph that answers the question on the lines provided. Use a topic sentence. Be sure to end every sentence with a period.

5. **Tell what would happen to the plants and animals if the water in a lake ecosystem were drained.**

_____

_____

_____

_____

_____

_____

_____

_____

Name_____   Date_____

Directions: Read the text below and study the diagram. Use information from both to help you answer the questions.

In any ecosystem, there are producers and consumers. Producers are living things that make their own food. Consumers are living things that eat other living things for food. In most ecosystems, the producers are plants. Plants get energy from sunlight and use it to produce their own food. Many animals consume, or eat, plants. When they eat plants, they consume the stored energy that the plants received from the sunlight.

1. **How do ALL consumers get energy?**
   - (A) making their own food
   - (B) growing and reproducing
   - (C) eating other living things
   - (D) hunting smaller animals

2. **How does energy move through an ecosystem?**
   - (F) sun ⟶ producers ⟶ consumers
   - (G) producers ⟶ consumers ⟶ sun
   - (H) consumers ⟶ producers ⟶ sun
   - (J) producers ⟶ sun ⟶ consumers

3. **Which of these is an example of a producer in a desert ecosystem?**
   - (A) bird
   - (B) coyote
   - (C) cactus
   - (D) insect

4. **How do producers get energy to grow?**
   - (F) plants
   - (G) hunting prey
   - (H) planting seeds
   - (J) making food

5. **Which of these is an example of a consumer?**
   - (A) flower
   - (B) vine
   - (C) tree
   - (D) monkey

GO ON

Name_____ Date_____

Directions: Study the diagram below. Use the information to help you answer the questions.

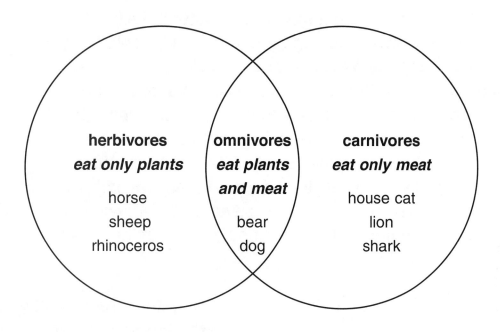

1. **Rabbits don't eat meat. In which section of the diagram does a rabbit belong?**
   - (A) herbivores
   - (B) omnivores
   - (C) carnivores
   - (D) all of the above

2. **Monkeys eat meat and plants. In which section of the diagram does a monkey belong?**
   - (F) herbivores
   - (G) omnivores
   - (H) carnivores
   - (J) all of the above

3. **Which of the following would a rhinoceros eat?**
   - (A) grass
   - (B) insects
   - (C) fish
   - (D) elephants

4. **Which of the following would a lion eat?**
   - (F) lettuce
   - (G) flowers
   - (H) fruit
   - (J) meat

Grade 3

Directions: Read the text below. Use the information to help you answer the questions.

Picture a tree that fell during a storm. Right after the storm, it still looks like a tree. Months later, it will be rotten and the wood will be soft. Ten years from now, the whole tree will be gone. What happened to it?

The tree decomposed. Some living things eat plants and animals that are already dead. These living things decompose, or break down, plants and animals that were once alive. They are called decomposers. Some mushrooms are decomposers. Some tiny living things called bacteria are also decomposers.

Animals that eat dead animals they did not kill are called scavengers. Vultures, hyenas, crabs, and even some ants are scavengers. Earthworms are scavengers that eat mainly plant material. It might sound yucky, but they keep the ecosystem clear of dead plants and animals.

1. **What does decompose mean?**
   - (A) die
   - (B) live
   - (C) break down
   - (D) scavenge

2. **A hyena is a scavenger. It _____ .**
   - (F) decomposes plants
   - (G) eats dead animals it did not kill
   - (H) stays far away from deadly decomposers
   - (J) hunts and kills animals, but doesn't eat them

3. **Which of the following will take the longest to decompose?**
   - (A) a pile of leaves
   - (B) a plastic bottle
   - (C) an eggshell
   - (D) a fallen tree branch

4. **A tree is most likely decomposing if _____ .**
   - (F) its flowers have fallen off
   - (G) it has mushrooms growing on it
   - (H) its leaves have turned brown
   - (J) it has bird nests in its branches

Name_____ Date_____

Directions: Read the text below and study the diagram. Use information from both to help you answer the questions.

HINT: Write your answers as neatly as you can on short-answer questions. If you cannot think of a word, draw it.

A food chain shows where the living things in an ecosystem get their food.

 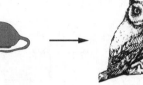

Sunflowers   Mouse   Owl

1. **In this food chain, what eats the plant?**
   - Ⓐ sunflower
   - Ⓑ mouse
   - Ⓒ owl
   - Ⓓ none of the above

2. **Which is the producer?**
   - Ⓕ bird
   - Ⓖ mouse
   - Ⓗ sunflower
   - Ⓙ owl

3. **What would happen to the caterpillar if you removed all plants from this ecosystem?**

   it would
   decompose
   _____

4. **Which food chain might you find in an ocean?**
   - Ⓐ sun ⟶ small fish ⟶ trout ⟶ bear
   - Ⓑ sun ⟶ plankton ⟶ small fish ⟶ penguin ⟶ seal
   - Ⓒ sun ⟶ cactus ⟶ pack rat ⟶ snake
   - Ⓓ sun ⟶ crab ⟶ small fish ⟶ seal ⟶ shark

GO ON

Name_____   Date_____

━━━━━━━━━━━ **Grade 3** ━━━━━━━━━━━

Directions: Study the food web below. Use the information to help you answer the questions.

HINT: Use your finger to trace the paths of the arrows. Think about what is happening in the diagram. What is it showing you?

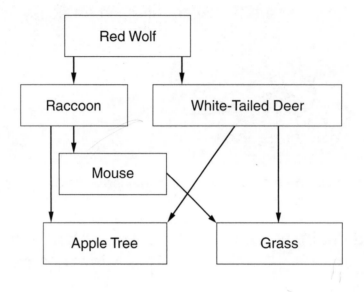

1. **What does a white-tailed deer eat in this ecosystem?**
   - (A) the grass and the mouse
   - (B) the red wolf and the apple tree
   - (C) the apple tree and the grass
   - (D) the grass and the raccoon

2. **What does the red wolf eat?**
   - (F) the mouse, the grass, and the sun
   - (G) the white-tailed deer and the grass
   - (H) the raccoon and the grass
   - (J) the raccoon and the white-tailed deer

3. **Where does the grass get energy to make its own food?**
   - (A) from the sun
   - (B) from the apple tree
   - (C) from the white-tailed deer and the mouse
   - (D) from the red wolf

4. **Which of these lists ALL the carnivores in the food web?**
   - (F) red wolf
   - (G) red wolf, raccoon
   - (H) raccoon, mouse, white-tailed deer
   - (J) raccoon, mouse, white-tailed deer, red wolf

Name_____ Date_____

Directions: Read the text below. Use the information to help you answer questions 1–3.

One of Alex's favorite activities to do on the weekends is hiking. She likes going for long walks and being in nature. While she's hiking, Alex also enjoys taking pictures. She uses her digital camera to photograph birds, trees, and clouds. But in some ways hiking can be dangerous. For instance, Alex needs to make sure she doesn't get lost. She can figure out where she is by using a map and compass. However, to use these tools she also needs landmarks like streams, fields, and rock formations.

1. **Name three objects in the passage that were created in nature.**

   tree, Clouds,
   birds

   _____

2. **Name three objects in the passage that were created by humans.**

   Map, copass, camera

   _____

   _____

3. **Explain why hunting endangered animals is a problem.**

   soIt you were hunting
   cheitas and you hunted
   too many they
   would get
   exitict and dinos
   are exitict.

   _____

   _____

Name_____ Date_____

Directions: Read the questions. Choose the truest possible answer. Shade in the circle before your choice.

1. **Which is an example of exercise?**
   - (A) jumping rope
   - (B) watching TV
   - (C) playing video games
   - (D) using the computer

2. **You can tell that exercise is making your heart stronger if it _____ .**
   - (F) makes you breathe fast
   - (G) uses your arms and legs
   - (H) makes your body feel sore
   - (J) involves an exercise machine

3. **Which helps build and repair tissue in your body?**
   - (A) protein
   - (B) muscle
   - (C) cells
   - (D) organs

4. **Why do you brush your teeth?**
   - (F) to tire you out so you can get ready for bed
   - (G) to keep your skin clean
   - (H) to keep you from talking too much
   - (J) to get rid of plaque and sugars that cause cavities

5. **Staying healthy and clean is also called having good _____ .**
   - (A) sanitation
   - (B) hygiene
   - (C) recycling
   - (D) dry cleaning

Directions: Read the questions. Write your answers on the lines provided.

6. **Describe two things you could do to eat better.**

   exercise and rest

   _____

7. **What are some things you do every day to stay healthy and clean?**

   exercise and take showers.

   _____

STOP

Name_____ Date_____

Grade 3

Directions: Read the questions. Choose the truest possible answer. Shade in the circle before your choice.

1. **Why is it important to recycle and conserve?**
   - (A) so we can feed everyone
   - (B) so we can have enough resources for everyone
   - (C) to save lives and help animals
   - (D) to make the world safer for everyone

2. **Which is an example of reusing?**
   - (F) turning newspaper into new white paper
   - (G) planting flowers and trees in a park
   - (H) turning the lights off in a room when you leave
   - (J) using an empty soup can to hold markers

3. **How does most paper get recycled?**
   - (A) It is cut, made into pulp, and flattened into new sheets.
   - (B) The sheets are all painted white and put back on the shelves of stores.
   - (C) It is put into a giant washing machine and then a huge dryer.
   - (D) It goes to a landfill with other trash.

4. **What does this symbol mean?**
   - (F) There is a cycle of life.
   - (G) The product can be recycled.
   - (H) There is a triangular pattern of particles.
   - (J) There is movement in the product.

5. **Which is one way to conserve water?**
   - (A) Measure it carefully.
   - (B) Fill up your bathtub once a day.
   - (C) Turn off water while you brush your teeth.
   - (D) Give your garden more water than it needs.

6. **Which is one way to conserve energy sources?**
   - (F) walk to school
   - (G) use a fireplace
   - (H) turn up the heat in your house
   - (J) keep the lights on when you leave a room

0-7696-8063-1—*Science Test Practice*

Content Standard D

Section D takes a more in-depth approach to the understanding of the earth, its materials, and how the planet fits in with the rest of the cosmos. Students will explore the solar system, including the various planets, comets, and asteroids. Students will also learn about the earth itself, including its physical features and layers, as well as how its cycles work together to maintain a balance that supports life.

Students will apply certain knowledge about the earth to gain a greater understanding of its various cycles. Included are erosion, precipitation, deposition, and natural disasters like landslides, earthquakes, volcanoes, and weather phenomena.

Section D gives students the opportunity to understand most of the basic processes that make life possible on the earth. Students can explain what makes the earth a special planet in our solar system and in the universe.

Name_____ Date_____

Grade 3

Directions: Read the questions. Choose the truest possible answer. Shade in the circle before your choice.

1. **Th earth is mostly shaped like a(n) _____ .**
   - Ⓐ ball
   - Ⓑ piece of paper
   - Ⓒ hose
   - Ⓓ egg

2. **One part of the earth we use for fuel is _____ .**
   - Ⓕ dirt
   - Ⓖ steel
   - Ⓗ salt water
   - Ⓙ coal

3. **Kelly decided to dig a hole in her backyard. "I'm going to dig to the other side of the earth," she announced. Her sister Flora said, "That's impossible." Why?**
   - Ⓐ There is no other side of the earth.
   - Ⓑ Kelly's shovel was too small to dig well.
   - Ⓒ The earth's core is too hot.
   - Ⓓ Flora was just teasing Kelly.

4. **One part of the earth we use as a building material is _____ .**
   - Ⓕ iron
   - Ⓖ water
   - Ⓗ oxygen
   - Ⓙ oil

Directions: Read the questions. Write your answers on the lines provided.

5. **When we look at th earth from space, much of it is blue. Why?**

   because of the oceans.

6. **The earth is protected from the heat of the sun by the atmosphere. What would happen to the earth if the atmosphere disappeared?**

   we would be flying all daylong from gravity.

STOP

Name_____ Date_____

Directions: Read the text below and study the diagram. Use words in the Word Bank to fill in the missing labels.

HINT: If you have seen a diagram before, but the one on the test looks different, don't panic. Draw the one you know next to the one in the book. Then you can compare them.

1. The earth has four layers. They are the crust, mantle, inner core, and outer core. All people can see from the earth is the crust. Soil, mountains, beaches, deserts, and the ocean floor are all part of the crust. Below the crust is the mantle. This is like the crust, but very hot because it is close to the outer core. The inner and outer cores are very, very hot. The inner core is in the middle of the earth.

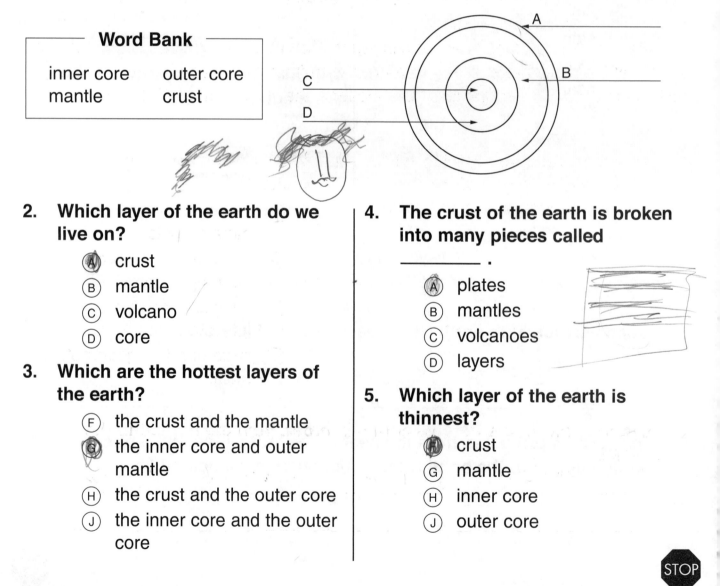

Word Bank

| inner core | outer core |
| mantle | crust |

2. **Which layer of the earth do we live on?**
   - Ⓐ crust
   - Ⓑ mantle
   - Ⓒ volcano
   - Ⓓ core

3. **Which are the hottest layers of the earth?**
   - Ⓕ the crust and the mantle
   - Ⓖ the inner core and outer mantle
   - Ⓗ the crust and the outer core
   - Ⓙ the inner core and the outer core

4. **The crust of the earth is broken into many pieces called**
   _____ .
   - Ⓐ plates
   - Ⓑ mantles
   - Ⓒ volcanoes
   - Ⓓ layers

5. **Which layer of the earth is thinnest?**
   - Ⓕ crust
   - Ⓖ mantle
   - Ⓗ inner core
   - Ⓙ outer core

STOP

Name_____ Date_____

Grade 3

Directions: Read the text below and study the diagram. Use information from both to help you answer the questions.

Rocks form over millions of years. Some may form after a volcano erupts and pours lava over the land. The lava cools and forms rock. These rocks are called igneous rocks.

Other rocks form when small pieces of rock, such as sand grains, are pressed so tightly that they become stuck together. Because they form from sediment, these rocks are called sedimentary rocks.

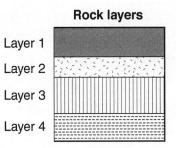
Rock layers
Layer 1
Layer 2
Layer 3
Layer 4

Rocks can also form when igneous or sedimentary rocks are heated or are pressed together under such tremendous pressure that they change. These rocks are called metamorphic rocks.

When rocks form, they often form in layers. Picture a lava flow. It spreads out and covers all the rocks below it. The rocks that form from the lava are newer than the rocks below them. If another lava flow happens, the rocks formed will be newer still.

1. **Based on what you read in the passage, which one of these rock layers would be the oldest?**
   - (A) Layer 1
   - (B) Layer 2
   - (C) Layer 3
   - (D) Layer 4

2. **What are the three types of rocks?**
   - (F) igneous, sedimentary, metamorphic
   - (G) igneous, metamorphic, geographic
   - (H) sedimentary, geographic, igneous
   - (J) metamorphic, geographic, mafic

3. **List the rock layers in the diagram in order, from the newest to the oldest.**

   metamorphic, ignious, sedimentry

Grade 3

Directions: Read the text below and study the diagram. Follow the arrows to see how the rocks change. Use information from both to help you answer the questions.

HINT: If you don't know a word, try to break it down. Does it sound like any other words you know? What word does "sedimentary" sound like?

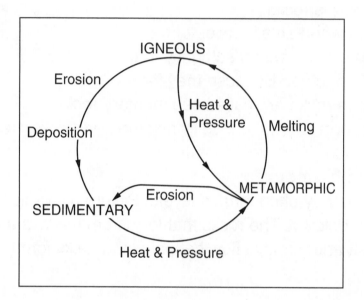

1. **When metamorphic rock melts and turns into magma, which rock will it become?**

   _____Sedimentary_____

2. **When igneous rocks are broken down into sediments, what form of rock will they become?**

   _____igneos_____

3. **Explain how metamorphic rock can become sedimentary rock.**

   When igneos and sediment
   rocks are pushed down sooo-
   -ooo hard with heat and
   preasure it tuns to
   metamorpihic rocks.

STOP

Name_____ Date_____

Directions: Study the diagram below. Use words in the Word Bank to fill in the missing labels.

1.

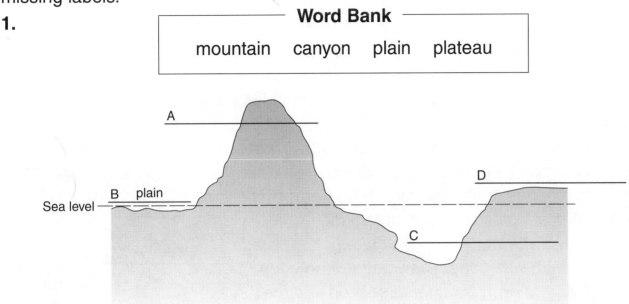

```
┌──────────────── Word Bank ────────────────┐
│                                            │
│    mountain   canyon   plain   plateau     │
│                                            │
└────────────────────────────────────────────┘
```

A _____

B   plain

Sea level

D _____

C _____

Directions: Read the question. Write your answers on the lines provided.

2.   **Give two more examples of landforms.**

_____ plain _____

_____ canyon _____

Directions: Read the questions. Choose the truest possible answer. Shade in the circle before your choice.

3.   **A mountain is _____ .**

Ⓐ a thin island near the coast

Ⓑ a deep valley with very steep sides

Ⓒ a flat area in the middle of the United States

Ⓓ a place on the earth much higher than the land around it

4.   **Which is a way a landform can change shape?**

Ⓕ A new bird species is discovered on a mountain.

Ⓖ A tree can fall down on a hillside.

Ⓗ People can level a hill to build houses.

Ⓙ Snow in a valley can melt.

GO ON

Directions: Read the text below and study the diagram. Use information from both to help you answer the questions.

Everyone in New Hampshire knew "The Old Man of the Mountain." It wasn't a person, though. It was a rock formation. Seen from the side, it looked like a man's face. It was one of the most famous landmarks in New England.

Five ledges of stone made up the Old Man. Three formed its forehead, nose, and chin. Since the 1800s people had stopped to see the rock. It was part of a cliff in the White Mountains, in a state park.

On May 3, 2003, workers in the state park noticed that the Old Man was gone. The weather had been windy and very rainy. The rain had seeped into the cracks in the rock. When the water froze, it split the rock. During the night, the rocks making up the forehead and nose broke off from the cliff.

1. **What was the "Old Man of the Mountain"?**
   - (A) a state park worker
   - (B) a rock formation
   - (C) a person who lived in the hills
   - (D) a fountain

2. **The forces that worked on the Old Man were causing _____ .**
   - (F) deposition
   - (G) summation
   - (H) weathering
   - (J) sedimentation

3. **What happened to the Old Man of the Mountain?**
   - (A) It collapsed and fell after bad weather.
   - (B) It got tired of looking and ran away.
   - (C) It was moved to another cliff by workers.
   - (D) It was bought by Massachusetts.

Name_____   Date_____

Grade 3

Directions: Read the questions. Choose the truest possible answer. Shade in the circle before your choice.

HINT: If you have to guess, try to eliminate one or two answers.

1. **A great deal of _____ might cause a flood.**
   - Ⓐ fire
   - Ⓑ sun
   - Ⓒ soil
   - Ⓓ rain

2. **Animals' homes might be flooded if they are near a _____ .**
   - Ⓕ river
   - Ⓖ forest
   - Ⓗ desert
   - Ⓙ mountain

3. **A landslide might be dangerous for animals that live _____ .**
   - Ⓐ in a lake
   - Ⓑ by a river
   - Ⓒ in a desert
   - Ⓓ on a mountain

4. **Which of these can cause a landslide?**
   - Ⓕ fire
   - Ⓖ gravity
   - Ⓗ the sun
   - Ⓘ animals

5. **Animals might try to move to higher ground in a flood because _____ .**
   - Ⓐ water moves downhill
   - Ⓑ they want a better view
   - Ⓒ moving keeps them warm
   - Ⓓ high ground is near the sun

6. **In which of these is damage caused mostly by wind?**
   - Ⓕ a flood
   - Ⓖ a tornado
   - Ⓗ a landslide
   - Ⓙ an earthquake

Name_____ Date_____

Directions: Study the diagram below. Use words in the Word Bank to fill in the missing labels.

1.

┌─────────────── **Word Bank** ───────────────┐
│   lava   ash   smoke   cone   │
└──┘

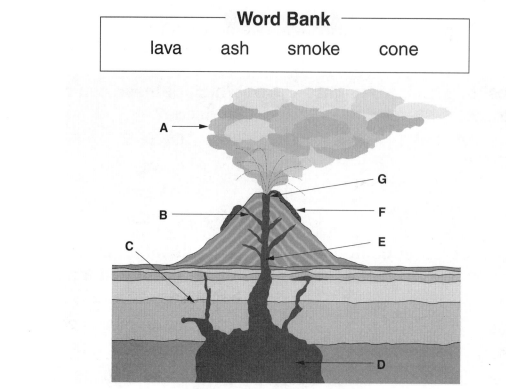

Directions: Read the questions. Choose the truest possible answer. Shade in the circle before your choice.

2. **After the volcano erupts, the lava will _____ .**

   Ⓐ cool and soften
   Ⓑ cool and harden
   Ⓒ heat up and soften
   Ⓓ heat up and harden

3. **A volcano's cone forms because _____ .**

   Ⓕ ash builds up over time
   Ⓖ dirt comes out of the volcano
   Ⓗ lava digs holes in the ground
   Ⓙ none of the above

4. **How might an earthquake affect animals?**

   Ⓐ All the animals on the earth would die after an earthquake.
   Ⓑ It gets very cold after an earthquake, so animals would freeze.
   Ⓒ Animals could lose their homes and food sources for a while.
   Ⓓ Animals are used to earthquakes and would not be affected at all.

GO ON

Grade 3

Directions: Read the questions. Choose the truest possible answer. Shade in the circle before your choice.

1. **Which process creates soil?**
   - Ⓐ overflow
   - Ⓑ digestion
   - Ⓒ weathering
   - ⓓ reproduction

2. **_____ create holes that let air get into the soil.**
   - Ⓕ Plants
   - Ⓖ Rocks
   - Ⓗ Animals
   - Ⓙ Minerals

3. **Most plants grow best in _____ .**
   - Ⓐ clay
   - Ⓑ sand
   - Ⓒ water
   - Ⓓ topsoil

Directions: Read the question. Write your answer on the line provided.

4. **Deepak has two pots of soil. In Pot A, the soil is dark and moist. In Pot B, the soil is light and dry. What is one thing that might make the pots of soil different?**

If a worm lived in pot B it would die because it is too dry and it could live in pot A because it is moist.

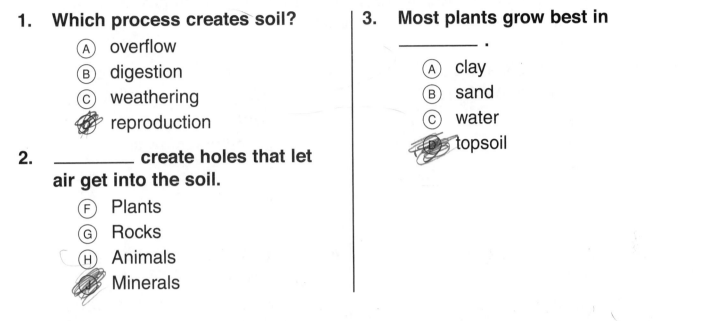

GO ON

Name_____ Date_____

Directions: Read the questions. Choose the truest possible answer. Shade in the circle before your choice.

HINT: If you are not sure of your answer, write a question mark next to it. Come back to the question when you have time.

1. **Which of the following can be found in the atmosphere?**
   - (A) water vapor
   - (B) rocks
   - (C) iron
   - (D) lava

2. **Air is a _____ of gases.**
   - (F) solution
   - (G) mixture
   - (H) volume
   - (J) layer

3. **A lot of air is made up of a gas called _____ , which we breathe.**
   - (A) carbon dioxide
   - (B) steam
   - (C) hydrogen
   - (D) oxygen

4. **Which of these causes air pollution?**
   - (F) skunks spraying predators
   - (G) fish swimming in a lake
   - (H) plants releasing seeds into the air
   - (J) cars burning gasoline

Directions: Read the questions. Write your answers on the lines provided.

5. **Air is invisible. Give two ways that you know it surrounds you.**

   You can breathe it in you
   can feel it.

6. **Radiation from the sun flows to the earth. The ozone layer protects the earth from harmful radiation. What would happen if there were no ozone layer?**

Name_____ Date_____

Directions: Read the questions. Choose the truest possible answer. Shade in the circle before your choice.

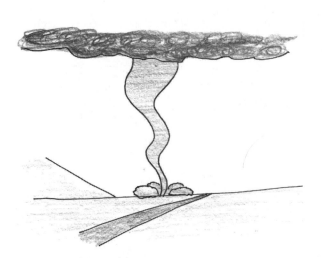

1. The weather event in the picture above is a(n) _____ .
- (A) blizzard
- (B) tornado
- (C) hurricane
- (D) thunderstorm

2. Which is an example of a weather event?
- (F) summer
- (G) rain forest
- (H) ocean
- (J) rainstorm

3. Which is the biggest danger from hurricanes?
- (A) falling ice
- (B) polluted air
- (C) strong winds
- (D) cold temperatures

Directions: Read the question. Write a paragraph that answers it on the lines provided. Use a topic sentence. Be sure to end every sentence with a period.

4. You are a meteorologist on the radio. Some people are angry at you when it rains. Write a letter to them explaining why it is not your fault.

It is not my fault because
the climate makes the choises
in ~~the~~ wiche it should rain or
not. So it is ~~never~~ not are
fault.

STOP

Directions: Read the questions. Choose the truest possible answer. Shade in the circle before your choice.

1. **Why do thunderstorms often occur in the spring and summer?**

    (A) The rain helps cool off the air.

    (B) Lightning comes from the sun.

    (C) Snow on the ground stops them.

    (D) Storms form when warm air rises.

2. **Which of these is the safest to do during a thunderstorm?**

    (F) stay inside a building

    (G) sit outside in a park

    (H) stand near a metal pole

    (J) stand on top of your house

3. **How are thunder and lightning related?**

    (A) Thunder reflects off clouds and makes lightning.

    (B) Thunder happens because of lightning.

    (C) Lightning always follows thunder.

    (D) Lightning is not related to thunder.

4. **Oliver sees a flash of lightning in the sky. He counts until he hears the sound of thunder. What is he trying to find out?**

    (F) where it will rain next

    (G) how much rain is coming

    (H) how close the storm is

    (J) if he is in immediate danger

Directions: Read the question. Write your answer on the line provided.

5. **Is lightning dangerous? Why or why not?**

    _____

    _____

6. **Is thunder dangerous? Why or why not?**

    _____

    _____

GO ON

Name_____   Date_____

Grade 3

Directions: Study the diagram below. Use words in the Word Bank to fill in the missing labels.

1.

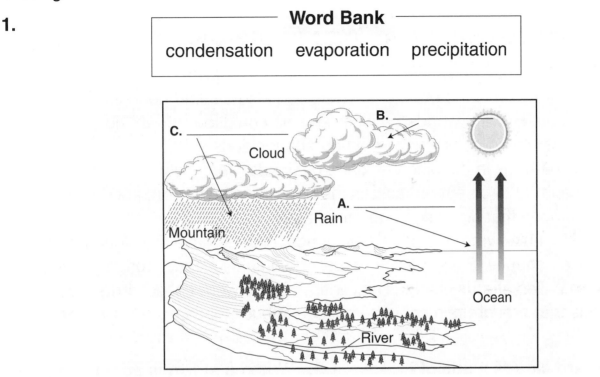

Word Bank

condensation   evaporation   precipitation

Directions: Read the questions. Choose the truest possible answer. Shade in the circle before your choice.

2. **What forms during condensation?**
    - (A) liquid water
    - (B) water vapor
    - (C) plant leaves
    - (D) carbon dioxide

3. **As the sun heats snow, snow changes from _____**
    - (F) solid to gas
    - (G) gas to solid
    - (H) liquid to gas
    - (J) solid to liquid

4. **Precipitation comes from the _____ in the sky.**
    - (A) sun
    - (B) stars
    - (C) Moon
    - (D) clouds

5. **Kathleen leaves an ice cube on the ground on a hot day. When she returns, the ice has become _____ .**
    - (F) rich soil
    - (G) liquid water
    - (H) water vapor
    - (J) carbon dioxide

STOP

Directions: Read the text below. Use the information to help you answer the questions.

Luke Howard: His Head Was in the Clouds

In 1783, London was covered in a thick, cold cloud called "the Great Fog." It was caused by two volcano eruptions. The cloud also caused beautiful sunsets. A boy named Luke Howard wondered what else he could learn from the cloud. In Luke's day, people did not know very much about clouds.

Luke saw patterns in the different kinds of clouds. Some were puffy and white, and some seemed to be spread across the sky. Some were dark and heavy. Some looked like stripes that didn't seem to move at all.

Later in life, Luke wrote a book about clouds. In it, he gave the clouds names based on their shapes. Puffy ones were called cumulus clouds. Long stripes of clouds were called stratus clouds. Thin, wispy clouds were called cirrus clouds. Dark clouds that brought rain could be called nimbus clouds.

1. **What are clouds made of?**
   - Ⓐ warm air
   - Ⓑ cold wind
   - Ⓒ sand and dust
   - Ⓓ water droplets

2. **What are four types of clouds?**

   cumules, states,
   cirrus,
   nimbus

3. **When a storm is coming, which kind of clouds are you likely to see?**
   - Ⓕ cirrus
   - Ⓖ cumulus
   - Ⓗ cumulo-cirrus
   - Ⓘ nimbus

4. **What did "the Great Fog" and clouds have to do with each other?**

   Ⓐ Fog and clouds are both made up of water droplets.

   Ⓑ Fog and clouds are both gray and rainy.

   Ⓒ Luke Howard wished both fog and rain would go away.

   Ⓓ Luke Howard named both the fog and the clouds.

5. **What will eventually happen to water vapor in a cloud?**

   Ⓕ It will evaporate.

   Ⓖ It will remain in the cloud.

   Ⓗ It will become precipitation.

   Ⓙ It will make oxygen.

6. **Give one way you can use clouds to predict the weather.**

   if they where gray and Puffy it would rain

Directions: Read the questions. Choose the truest possible answer. Shade in the circle before your choice.

1. **Leslie would like to go skiing and snowboarding. What kind of climate should she visit?**
   - Ⓐ hot, dry climate
   - Ⓑ cold, dry climate
   - Ⓒ mild, wet climate
   - Ⓓ cold, wet climate

2. **Trace's friend Angelo went to visit Trace in Texas. Trace told Angelo that he lived in a hot, dry climate. When Angelo stepped off the plane, he saw that there was light snow on the ground. What happened?**
   - Ⓕ Sometimes the weather is very different than a general climate.
   - Ⓖ Trace was wrong about Texas's climate.
   - Ⓗ Texas has a climate that changes every single day.
   - Ⓙ Climates can never be used to predict what the weather will be.

3. **Who would probably care MOST about large changes in climate?**
   - Ⓐ a cashier
   - Ⓑ a farmer
   - Ⓒ a teacher
   - Ⓓ a chef

Directions: Read the questions. Write your answers on the lines provided.

4. **Tell one way that climate is different from weather.**

   _____

   _____

   _____

5. **Your pen pal wants to know about the climate where you live. Write a letter describing it.**

   _____

   _____

   _____

   _____

   _____

   _____

   _____

   _____

   _____

   _____

   _____

Grade 3

Directions: Read the questions. Choose the truest possible answer. Shade in the circle before your choice.

1. The water in rivers, lakes, and streams is called fresh water because it has no _____ .
   - (A) fish
   - (B) salt
   - (C) soil
   - (D) pollution

2. Where would it be the most difficult to get fresh water?
   - (F) in a forest
   - (G) in a desert
   - (H) near a lake
   - (J) near a river

3. Which animal would you find naturally in a freshwater ecosystem?
   - (A) whale
   - (B) chicken
   - (C) octopus
   - (D) beaver

4. Snow _____ before it becomes part of a river, lake, or stream.
   - (F) melts
   - (G) boils
   - (H) freezes
   - (J) evaporates

Directions: Read the question. Write your answer on the line provided.

5. What is one resource found in the ocean?

_____

6. Why can pollution in the ocean be a problem?

_____

7. "If I was trapped on an island in the middle of the ocean, I would have nothing to drink," said Mitsuru. Would Mitsuru have water to drink? Why or why not?

_____

_____

GO ON

Name_____ Date_____

Directions: Read the text below and study the diagram. Use information from both to help you answer the questions.

HINT: If you are asked to give the meaning of a word, go back to the passage. Circle the word in the passage and see if you can find the meaning.

Imagine that you are holding a marshmallow. Now you take a stick and poke it through the marshmallow so that it comes out the other end. You can make the marshmallow spin by rolling the stick between two fingers.

The earth has an imaginary stick through its center called an axis. It begins at the North Pole and goes through the earth until it reaches the South Pole. When the earth rotates, or spins, we say that it spins on its axis.

Rotation is not the only way the earth moves. It also revolves, or moves in a circle, around the sun.

1. **What does the word *rotate* mean?**
   - Ⓐ poke through
   - Ⓑ spin
   - Ⓒ roll
   - Ⓓ move in a circle

2. **What does the word *revolve* mean?**
   - Ⓕ poke through
   - Ⓖ spin
   - Ⓗ roll
   - Ⓙ move in a circle

3. **Enrique watches a merry-go-round at the park. All of the horses spin around a center pole. The pole acts just like the earth's _____ .**
   - Ⓐ North Pole
   - Ⓑ South Pole
   - Ⓒ axis
   - Ⓓ revolution

4. **Planets and dwarf planets _____ around the sun.**
   - Ⓕ revolve
   - Ⓖ axis
   - Ⓗ pole
   - Ⓙ rotate

Name_____   Date_____

Directions: Study the diagram below. Use information from it to help you answer the questions.

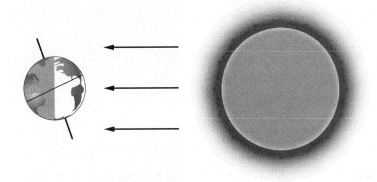

EARTH   SUN

1. **If the earth stopped rotating, what would happen to day and night?**

   Ⓐ They would last twice as long.

   Ⓑ There would always be day, or always be night.

   Ⓒ No part of the world would have day.

   Ⓓ No part of the world would have night.

2. **How long does it take for the earth to rotate on its axis?**

   Ⓕ 1 hour

   Ⓖ 24 hours

   Ⓗ 7 days

   Ⓙ 365 days

3. **If South Africa is faced away from the sun right now, what time might it be there?**

   Ⓐ morning

   Ⓑ noon

   Ⓒ afternoon

   Ⓓ midnight

4. **Seasons are caused by _____.**

   Ⓕ the tilt of the earth's axis

   Ⓖ the moon's gravitational pull

   Ⓗ the sun's changing strength

   Ⓙ the distance between the earth and the sun

Name_____ Date_____

Grade 3

Directions: Study the diagram below. Use your pencil to put an X on each inner planet.

1.

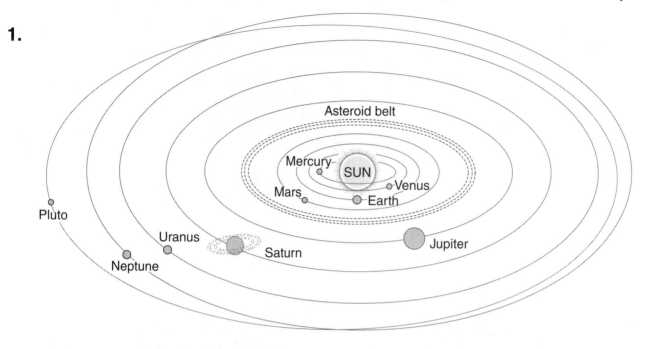

Directions: Read the questions. Choose the truest possible answer. Shade in the circle before your choice.

2. **Most of the outer planets and dwarf planets are much _____ than the inner planets and dwarf planets.**
   - Ⓐ bigger
   - Ⓑ smaller
   - Ⓒ denser
   - Ⓓ lighter

3. **The sun looks so much bigger than other stars because it is _____ .**
   - Ⓕ a ball of gas
   - Ⓖ a yellow star
   - Ⓗ closest to the earth
   - Ⓙ the largest star ever

4. **Which of the following planets has an orbit nearest to the earth's orbit?**
   - Ⓐ Mars
   - Ⓑ Pluto
   - Ⓒ Mercury
   - Ⓓ Jupiter

5. **Which is the largest object in the solar system?**
   - Ⓕ the earth
   - Ⓖ Jupiter
   - Ⓗ the sun
   - Ⓙ the moon

GO ON

Name_____ Date_____

Directions: Study the diagram below. Use words in the Word Bank to fill in the missing labels.

1.

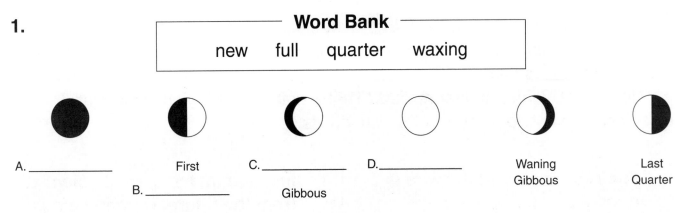

Word Bank

new   full   quarter   waxing

A._____   First   C._____   D._____   Waning   Last
                                                                Gibbous   Quarter
                B._____   Gibbous

Directions: Read the questions. Choose the truest possible answer. Shade in the circle before your choice.

2. **When the part of the moon facing the earth is completely lit, it is a _____ .**
   - (A) full moon
   - (B) new moon
   - (C) waning moon
   - (D) waxing moon

3. **Akar sees a new moon. About how long will it be until the moon is full?**
   - (F) 4 days
   - (G) 2 weeks
   - (H) 1 month
   - (J) 1 year

4. **Why would an astronaut have a hard time breathing on the moon without a spacesuit?**
   - (A) There is not enough air.
   - (B) There is not enough gravity.
   - (C) It is too cold.
   - (D) It is covered in water.

5. **The moon is mostly made of _____ .**
   - (F) helium
   - (G) rock
   - (H) chalk
   - (J) water

GO ON

Name_____ Date_____

Directions: Read the text below. Use the information to help you answer questions 1–3.

"Look at this electric wire," said Lian's mother. "See the rubber that covers it?"

"Yes," Lian answered. "But part of the rubber is worn away. You can see the wire sticking out of it. Is that safe?"

"No, it's not," Lian's mother replied. "That's exactly why I'm taking it to an electrical repair shop. They'll fix the wire so it's safe."

1. The rubber around the wire is a good _____ .
   - (A) conductor
   - (B) insulator
   - (C) resistance
   - (D) current

2. Why does Lian's mother think the wire is not safe?

   _____

   _____

   _____

   _____

3. Imagine that you are a scientist from the future. Human beings are already living on Mars. Your job is to create a way for people to survive on Mercury. Describe an invention that will help solve your problem.

   _____

   _____

   _____

   _____

   _____

   _____

   _____

   _____

GO ON

Name_____ Date_____

Directions: Study the diagram below. Use the information to help you answer questions 4–8.

Sunflowers   Mouse   Owl

4. **What is the figure an example of?**
   - (F) classification chart
   - (G) growth chart
   - (H) food web
   - (J) food chain

5. **In this diagram, the _____ must be a producer.**
   - (A) owl
   - (B) mouse
   - (C) sunflower
   - (D) sun

6. **If many people began to hunt owls, what would happen to the mouse population?**

_____

_____

_____

_____

_____

Directions: Read the questions. Choose the truest possible answer. Shade in the circle before your choice.

7. **What kind of rock might form at an erupting volcano?**
   - (F) igneous
   - (G) metamorphic
   - (H) eroded
   - (J) sedimentary

8. **The hot, melted rock that comes out of a volcano is called _____ .**
   - (A) lava
   - (B) sedimentary
   - (C) igneous
   - (D) humus

GO ON

Name_____ Date_____

Directions: Read the text below and study the chart. Use information from both to help you answer questions 9–11.

For an entire year, Chen did an experiment. He recorded his data in the graph below. Use the graph to answer the following questions.

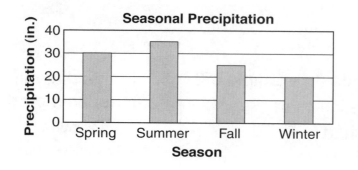

9. **What did Chen's experiment measure?**

- (F) tree and plant growth
- (G) snowfall and rainfall
- (H) wind and water speed
- (J) evaporation and condensation rates

10. **Which tool did Chen probably use in his experiment?**

- (A) microscope
- (B) balance
- (C) measuring cup
- (D) telescope

11. **Chen wants to make a table from his graph. Fill in the missing information.**

Seasonal Precipitation

Season	Precipitation (in)
Spring	
Summer	35 in
Fall	
Winter	

GO ON

Name_____ Date_____

Directions: Read the questions. Choose the truest possible answer. Shade in the circle before your choice.

12. **What causes the phases of the moon?**

   - (F) The earth casts a shadow on the moon.
   - (G) The sun casts a shadow on the moon.
   - (H) The sun lights up different parts of the moon.
   - (J) Different parts of the moon face the earth.

13. **Neptune _____ around the sun.**

   - (A) rotates
   - (B) axes
   - (C) revolves
   - (D) phases

14. **_____ is the only star in our solar system.**

   - (F) Jupiter
   - (G) The moon
   - (H) The sun
   - (J) Alpha Centauri

15. **Which is one thing a flower, an oak tree, and moss have in common?**

   - (A) They make their own food using the sun's energy.
   - (B) They are complex plants.
   - (C) They have tubes that carry water and nutrients.
   - (D) They can survive in a desert ecosystem.

16. **Most energy on the earth comes from _____.**

   - (F) the sun
   - (G) oxygen
   - (H) carbon dioxide
   - (J) humans

17. **Soil is an example of a _____ .**

   - (A) solution
   - (B) solvent
   - (C) millimeter
   - (D) mixture

18. **Chava turns off the lights as she leaves the room. She is _____ electricity.**

   - (F) conserving
   - (G) recycling
   - (H) reusing
   - (J) conducting

GO ON

Grade 3 Posttest

Directions: Read the question. Write your answer on the line provided.

19. **Nahma woke up early in the morning and pulled on a sweater to keep warm. By lunchtime, Nahma was so hot she had to take off her sweater. Why did that happen?**

_____

_____

_____

_____

20. **What is one difference between climate and weather?**

_____

_____

Directions: Read the text below. Use the information to help you answer questions 21 and 22.

"Why do you put salt in water before you boil it?" Levi asked his father.

"I'm not sure," his father admitted. "That's just what the instructions say to do."

"I wonder why it's so important," Levi said. "Maybe salt helps the water boil. Could that be true, Dad?"

"It could be," his father answered. "Why don't you find out?"

21. **What was Levi's hypothesis?**

_____

_____

22. **How can Levi test his hypothesis? (Make sure to include the tools he will use at each stage in his experiment.)**

_____

_____

_____

STOP

ANSWER KEY

Page 10 Pretest
1. A
2. F
3. A
4. H
5. B

Page 11 Pretest
6. J
7. D
8. G
9. D
10. J
11. A

Page 12 Pretest
12. D
13. H
14. A
15. G
16. Ex: size, shape, color, texture
17. Ex: walk, save water, recycle paper and cans

Page 13 Pretest
18. Answer should show understanding of the boundaries of a given ecosystem. Student should be able to tell what some of the natural flora, fauna, and land features are, if applicable.
19. Answer should include a driving question about the lamp, such as "Is it on a timer?" or "Does someone shut it off?" or "Is it motion- or light-activated?" Student should turn the question into a hypothesis and develop an experiment to test it, such as recording the times and looking for a pattern or running under it to test motion-sensitivity.

Page 14 Pretest
20. D
21. F
22. D

Page 16
1. C
2. J

Page 17
1. question → hypothesis → experiment → theory
2. If you don't have a question in mind, you don't know what factors to look for or what specific information to find.

3. Karen's idea is a hypothesis. She has not tested her hypothesis, and it is not proven yet.
4. A
5. H

Page 18
1. C
2. H
3. B

Page 19
1. B
2. F
3. C
4. F
5. D
6. F

Page 20
1. C
2. G
3. C
4. H
5. B
6. F

Page 21
1. the blocks
2. C
3. The carton of milk would have the same mass off the balance as it did on the balance. Mass is not affected by the balance.
4. F
5. D

Page 22
1. B
2. J
3. Ex: It is important to know temperature in order to know how to dress for the day, to see if things like food or candies will melt, or to makes sure that things being cooked or baked don't burn.
4. C
5. G

Page 23
1. A
2. G
3. They can find the volume using a measuring cup.
4. because water does not have a definite shape

Page 24
1. B

2. H
3. B
4. F
5. Ex: thermometer, magnifying glass; answer should not include tools for construction
6. Ex: satellite, telescope; answer should not include tools for construction

Page 25
1. Students should draw bar to 800.
2. Students should draw bar to 500.
3. Students should draw bar to 800.
4. Students should draw bar to 700.
5. Students should draw bar to 1400.
6. D

Page 26
1. A
2. F
3. A

Page 28
1. B
2. F
3. D
4. G
5. D

Page 29
1. A
2. G
3. C
4. F

Page 30
1. C
2. J
3. B
4. H
5. A
6. J

Page 31
1. C
2. G
3. A
4. F
5. A
6. G

Page 32
1. C
2. G
3. A
4. F
5. C

Page 33
1. stored
2. the sun
3. Fossil fuels
4. heat
5. A
6. J
7. D

Page 34
1. C
2. F
3. The light shines through a curved or round surface in all directions in a bulb. In a flashlight, all the light is directed forward.

Page 35
4. B
5. G
6. D
7. F

Page 36
1. B
2. F
3. C
4. J
5. because they come from fossils of plants and dead animals
6. Ex: wind, sun, running water, wood

Page 37
1. Ex: the ball hitting the bat, the ball being pitched, players running or sliding, hand signals
2. B
3. J
4. B
5. F
6. A

Page 39
1. Animals need to eat food to get energy, but plants can make their own food.
2. because frogs and other animals can be green, too
3. Ex: Plants cannot move around like animals can.

Page 40
1. C
2. H
3. D
4. F
5. Calvin forgot that plants need air to grow.

Page 41
1. flower
2. leaves
3. stem
4. roots
5. G
6. D
7. J
8. C

Page 42
1. A
2. F
3. B
4. F
5. Ex: animals carry the seed on their coats, birds eat the seeds and pass them through their digestive system, water carries them away, wind carries them away
6. seed → seedling → plant

Page 43
1. D
2. F
3. D
4. G
5. from eating food
6. When an animal species is extinct, it means that there are no more of that animal.

Page 44
1. A eyes; B gills; C fin; D tail
2. G
3. B
4. Poisons can get into fishes' bodies through their gills or mouth. The poisons can kill fish or make them sick.

Page 45
1. C
2. J
3. A
4. J
5. C

Page 46
1. C
2. F
3. C
4. J
5. Ex: hatch babies from eggs, are both vertebrates
5. Ex: feathers help some birds fly, protect them, and keep them warm

Page 47
1. A
2. J
3. C
4. G
5. A
6. Most mammals don't lay eggs and they have fur or hair.

Page 48
1. C
2. F
3. C
4. H
5. An elephant is too large to support its body without an internal skeleton.

Page 49
1. D
2. F
3. B
4. F
5. A
6. H

Page 50
1. lay eggs
2. fertilized
3. born
4. reproduce

Page 51
1. C
2. J
3. A
4. H
5. Ex: porcupine quills, claws, stripes

Page 52
1. A egg; B tadpole; C young frog; D adult frog
2. B
3. F

Page 53
1. C
2. G
3. B
4. F
5. C
6. Ex. There would be more animals in the forest with lots of water. Water is very important to all animals.

Page 54
1. C
2. G

Page 55

3. A
4. H
5. Answer should reflect understanding of how the lake supports the animals and plants. The plants might dry up because they can't get enough water, and the fish and aquatic life would die. Other animals who used the lake as a drinking source might relocate to find other water sources.

Page 56

1. C
2. F
3. C
4. J
5. D

Page 57

1. A
2. G
3. A
4. J

Page 58

1. C
2. G
3. B
4. G

Page 59

1. B
2. H
3. The caterpillar would die because it would have nothing to eat.
4. B

Page 60

1. C
2. J
3. A
4. G

Page 61

1. birds, trees, fields
2. digital camera, map, compass
3. When an animal is endangered, there are few of them left. Hunting them may remove the species from the world altogether.

Page 62

1. A
2. F
3. A
4. J
5. B

6. Ex: eat fresh foods, eat fewer sweets
7. Ex: bathe, wash hands

Page 63

1. B
2. J
3. A
4. G
5. C
6. F

Page 65

1. A
2. J
3. C
4. F
5. because most of the earth is covered by water
6. The sun would cause the earth to get too hot for life to continue to exist.

Page 66

1. A crust; B mantle; C inner core; D outer core
2. A
3. J
4. A
5. F

Page 67

1. D
2. F
3. Layer 1; Layer 2; Layer 3; Layer 4

Page 68

1. igneous rock
2. sedimentary rocks
3. These rocks break down into sediments. The sediments get cemented together and turn into sedimentary rock.

Page 69

1. A mountain; B plain; C canyon; D plateau
2. Ex: valleys, hills
3. D
4. H

Page 70

1. B
2. H
3. A

Page 71

1. D
2. F
3. A

4. G
5. D
6. G

Page 72

1. A smoke; B ash; C lava; D cone
2. B
3. F
4. C

Page 73

1. C
2. H
3. D
4. Pot A's soil contains more water than Pot B's soil does.

Page 74

1. A
2. G
3. D
4. J
5. Ex: You can breathe it and you can feel wind.
6. Ex: The radiation would be too hot and it would burn our skin.

Page 75

1. B
2. J
3. C
4. Answer should show understanding of what causes weather patterns. Response should make reference to the water cycle, areas of high and low pressure, or position of the earth in relation to the sun.

Page 76

1. D
2. F
3. B
4. H
5. Yes, because it is very hot, electrically charged air, and it can burn us.
6. No, because it is a sound that air makes when it moves quickly.

Page 77

1. A evaporation; B condensation; C precipitation
2. A
3. J
4. D
5. G

Page 78

1. D
2. stratus, cumulus, cirrus, and nimbus
3. J

Page 79

4. A
5. H
6. Ex: If you see nimbus clouds, it might rain; or if the clouds are moving quickly, a storm may be coming.

Page 80

1. D
2. F
3. B
4. Weather is the current conditions in an area, and climate is the general conditions over a period of time of a given place.
5. Answer should reflect understanding of seasonal shifts in climate and general temperatures of where he or she lives.

Page 81

1. B
2. G
3. D
4. F
5. Ex: fish, salt
6. Ex: It might harm fish or other living things in the ocean.
7. No, because people cannot safely drink seawater.

Page 82

1. B
2. J
3. C
4. F

Page 83

1. B
2. G
3. D
4. F

Page 84

1. Students should place an "x" on Mercury, Venus, Earth, and Mars.
2. A
3. H
4. A
5. H

Page 85

1. A new; B quarter; C waxing; D full

2. A
3. G
4. A
5. G

Page 86 Posttest

1. B
2. The exposed electrical wires can start a fire.
3. Answer should show understanding that the invention will need to combat heat and get air.

Page 87 Posttest

4. J
5. C
6. Ex. There would be no predator for the mouse. There would be too many mice.
7. F
8. A

Page 88 Posttest

9. G
10. C
11. Spring: 30 in.; Fall: 25 in.; Winter: 20 in.

Page 89 Posttest

12. F
13. C
14. H
15. A
16. F
17. D
18. F

Page 90 Posttest

19. At lunchtime, the sun is high in the sky. It heats up the earth and makes Nahma hot.
20. Climate is the weather over a certain amount of time in a specific place.
21. Maybe salt helps the water boil.
22. Answer should include these basic steps: Put two different pots on the same stove. Fill them equally with water (measuring cup). Measure some salt and put it in one of the pots. Turn up the stove to the same temperature. At specific intervals, use a thermometer to measure the temperatures. Record the temperatures and compare them.